PROCEEDINGS OF
THE 2013 INTERNATIONAL CONFERENCE ON
ENGINEERING OF RECONFIGURABLE SYSTEMS &
ALGORITHMS

ERSA 2013

Editor

Toomas P. Plaks

WORLDCOMP'13
July 22-25, 2013
Las Vegas Nevada, USA
www.world-academy-of-science.org

©CSREA Press

This volume contains papers presented at The 2013 International Conference on Engineering of Reconfigurable Systems & Algorithms (ERSA'13). Their inclusion in this publication does not necessarily constitute endorsements by editors or by the publisher.

ERSA'13
ENGINEERING OF RECONFIGURABLE SYSTEMS AND ALGORITHMS

The international conference on Engineering of Reconfigurable Systems and Algorithms (ERSA) was founded in 2001 and, since then, has been held each year in Las Vegas.

ERSA explores emerging trends and novel ideas in the area of parallel, reconfigurable, heterogeneous, high-performance computing architecture, design methods and applications. ERSA is promoting multidisciplinary research and new visionary approaches including bio-inspired architectures, computational biology, physics etc.

Since 2012, ERSA brings a new emphasis on the commercial and industrial challenges in preparing commercial applications for systems using reconfigurable, heterogeneous technology.

The proceedings of the ERSA Conference have been approved, by the evaluation board of science citation index (SCI) databases, for indexing, integrating, and inclusion into Elsevier indexing databases (Elsevier indexing databases include, among others: Scopus, SCI Compendex, Engineering Village, EMBASE, and others)

ERSA conference focuses on different approaches in engineering of reconfigurable systems: in hardware design and in implementing of algorithms; including theory, architecture, algorithms, design systems and applications that demonstrate the benefits of reconfigurable computing. ERSA conference solicits papers from broad area, from all aspects of reconfigurable heterogeneous computing, from simple applications on programmable logic to complex, intelligent, high-performance, embedded systems implemented as multicore systems and heterogeneous parallel processing systems. All these complex systems involve reconfigurability on software and/or hardware level.

The range of topics covers theory, architecture, algorithms, design systems, and applications that demonstrate the benefits of reconfigurable computing:
- Theory - Synthesis, Mapping, Parallelization, Partitioning...
- Software – CAD Systems and Languages, Compilers, Operating Systems...
- Hardware - Adaptive and Dynamic Hardware, Heterogeneous and Reconfigurable Architectures...
- Applications – HPC, Mobile Computing, Automotive Industry, Space and Military, Smart Cameras...

ERSA conference brings together leading scientists and researchers from academia and industry. ERSA is aiming to provide a forum where new research results can be quickly published and presented to research community, where people can discuss and share the latest ideas without a long publishing time. Only one and half months are required from submitting a paper to presenting it at the conference when following late CFP option. Late papers, which are not ready for conference time publication, are published in post-conference proceedings, in the official ERSA proceedings. All conference proceedings/books are considered for inclusion in major database indexes.

After the conference, best ERSA papers are published in special issues of reputable international journals: in The Journal of Supercomputing (Springer), IEEE TVLSI, ACM Transactions on Embedded Computing Systems.

This year, to support young and talented, ERSA launched the contest for "ERSA - NVIDIA Best Young Entrepreneur Award". The Award is devoted for entrepreneurs developing tools, advanced technologies and opportunities for supporting applications, both academic and commercial, across broad area of high-performance, embedded systems implemented as multicore systems and reconfigurable heterogeneous parallel processing systems.

I hope that the ERSA conference, covering different aspects of reconfiguration techniques and heterogeneous computing systems, will raise your awareness about the scope of reconfigurable (or adaptive) heterogeneous computing.

I would like to thank the authors for submitting their papers to ERSA'13 and for preparing the final versions of their papers for due date. I hope you all will have successful and enjoyable meeting in Las Vegas this year and I hope to meet you again in next years. I would like to extend my deepest gratitude for the efforts extended by the ERSA'13 Program Committee and to all external reviewers for their careful reading of all of the submitted papers.

Last but not least, I would like to thank the organizing team of The 2013 World Congress in Computer Science, Computer Engineering, and Applied Computing, and, especially, the General Chair Prof. Hamid Arabnia, for the continuous support and help in organizing the ERSA conference.

Toomas P. Plaks
ERSA Chairman
London
June, 2013

ERSA 2013 Conference Organization

Conference Chair

Dr. Toomas P. Plaks
London, UK

Academic and Industrial Advisory Board

- Mr. Lindsay M Black, MIET, MIEEE, IT & Technical Solution Sales, UK
- Mr. Steve Casselman, Principal Engineer at Altera Corporation, USA
- Dr. Alan Coppola, Principal, OptNgn Software, USA
- Mr. Jaime Cummins, President and CEO at Pico Computing; Founder and CEO of Edison Labs, USA
- Mr. Brian Durwood, CEO at Impulse Accelerated Technologies, USA
- Prof. Michael Flynn, Stanford University, USA
- Mr. Ty Garibay, VP of Embedded Processing at Altera, USA
- Dr. Steven Guccione, VP Senior Technology Manager, Bank of America, USA
- Mr. Daniel Nenni, Founder at The Semiconductor Wiki Project, USA
- Prof. Simon See, Director at Nvidia, Singapore; Professor of Shanghai Jiao Tong University, China
- Mr. Yousef Shemisa, CTO, Accurate Always, USA
- Dr. Eric Stahlberg, President, OpenFPGA, USA
- Mr. John Swan, EDATechForce, LLC , IEEE - Computer Society, EDPS Chair/Liason, Santa Clara Valley CS, IEEE
- Dr. Nick Tredennick, Gilder Technology Report, USA

ERSA-NVIDIA Award Committee

Leading Universities

- Prof. Michael Flynn, Stanford University, USA
- Prof. Wayne Luk, Imperial College London, UK
- Prof. Joerg Henkel, Karlsruhe Institute of Technology, Germany
- Prof. Hideharu Amano, Keio University, Japan
- Prof. Simon See, Shanghai Jiao Tong University, China

Leading Companies

- Mr. Can Ozdoruk, NVIDIA, Product Manager, USA
- Mr. Steve Casselman, Altera Corporation, Principal Engineer, USA
- Mr. Hugo Andrade, National Instruments, Principal Architect, USA

Steering Committee

- Prof. Stephan Brown, Univ.of Toronto, Canada
- Dr. Steven A. Guccione, CMPWare Inc., USA
- Prof. Masanori Hariyama, Tohoku University, Japan
- Prof. Wayne Luk, Imperial College, UK
- Prof. Bernard Pottier, Univ. of Bretagne Occidentale, France
- Dr. Eric Stahlberg, President, OpenFPGA, USA

Technical Program Committee

- Prof. Hideharu Amano, Keio Univ., Japan
- Prof. Paul Beckett, RMIT Univ., Australia
- Prof. Gabriel Caffarena, Universidad CEU San Pablo, Spain
- Prof. Guy Gogniat, Univ. of South Brittany, France
- Dr. Marek Gorgon, AGH Univ. of Technology, Poland
- Prof. Victor Goulart, Kyushu Univ., Japan
- Dr. Steven Guccione, Cmpware, USA
- Dr. Botella Guillermo, Complutense Univ. of Madrid, Spain
- Dr. Yajun Ha, National Univ. of Singapore, Singapore
- Prof. Masanori Hariyama, Tohoku Univ., Japan
- Dr. Jim Harkin, Univ. of Ulster, Northern Ireland
- Prof. Martin Herbordt, Boston Univ., USA
- Dr. Ju-wook Jang, Sogang Univ., Korea
- Dr. Kimmo Järvinen, Helsinki Univ. of Technology, Finland
- Prof. Jack Jean, Wright State Univ. Dayton, USA
- Dr. Paris Kitsos, Hellenic Open Univ., Greece
- Prof. Jaehwan John Lee, Purdue Univ., USA
- Prof. Jeong A Lee, Chosun Univ., S. Korea
- Prof. Miriam Leeser, Northeastern Univ., USA
- Dr. Andrés Otero, Universidad Politécnica de Madrid, Spain
- Prof. Cameron Patterson, Virginia Tech., USA
- Dr. Christian Pilato, Politecnico di Milano, Italy
- Dr. Mario Porrmann, Bielefeld Univ., Germany
- Prof. Bernard Pottier, Univ. of Bretagne Occidentale, France
- Prof. William H. Robinson, Vanderbilt Univ., USA

- Dr. Guido Rotondi, Italian National Statistical Institute (ISTAT), Italy
- Prof. Sergei Sawitzki, Univ. of Applied Sciences, The Netherlands
- Dr. Bala Sethuraman, Calypto Design Systems, USA
- Prof. Christian Siemers, Univ. of Applied Sciences Nordhausen, Germany
- Dr. Melissa C. Smith, Clemson Univ., USA
- Dr. Eric Stahlberg, OpenFPGA, USA
- Dr. Vivek Venugopal, National Solar Observatory, New Mexico, USA
- Prof. Sotirios G. Ziavras, New Jersey Institute of Technology, USA
- Prof. Peter Zipf, Universität Kassel, Germany

ERSA 2013 Partner Organizations

Parallella Community

Supercomputing for
Everyone

StreamComputing

Performance Engineers

ERSA 2013 Corporate Partners & Sponsors

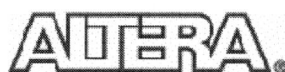

Contents

SESSION: BEST YOUNG ENTREPRENEUR; STUDENT RESEARCH
CATEGORY

SESSION: INVITED LECTURE

SESSION

COMMUNICATION TECHNIQUES IN RECONFIGURABLE SYSTEMS

Chair(s)

TBA

Hardware Parallel Decoder of Compressed HTTP Traffic on Service-oriented Router

Daigo Hogawa[1], Shin-ichi Ishida[1], Hiroaki Nishi[1]
[1] Dept. of Science and Technology, Keio University, Japan

Abstract—*This paper proposes a parallel GZIP decoder architecture that includes a multiple context manager for decompressing network streams directly on a router. On the Internet, some HTTP packet streams are encoded by GZIP. Moreover, Internet content is often divided into smaller packets and transmitted without regard to the original order of the packets. The previously proposed Service-oriented Router for content-based packet stream processing needs to decode GZIP data in order to analyze packet payloads. The proposed GZIP decoder is implemented in hardware in order to process the data of multiple network data streams quickly and concurrently using context switching. The GZIP decoding hardware logic is simulated by Verilog-HDL. When one dictionary generation module and eight decoding modules are designed using FPGA, the throughput becomes 0.71 Gbps. When this architecture is synthesized in ASIC, the throughput reaches 10.41 Gbps and the circuit area of that architecture becomes $0.14mm^2$.*

Keywords: GZIP, Decompression, Hardware, Parallel, Context Switch, Service-oriented Router.

1. Introduction

Internet technology has made great progress in the last decade. Since it is now used as a communication tool throughout the world, the amount of the data transmitted over the network has been increasing. People have come to use the Internet not only for collecting information, but also for transmitting it. Recently, people have begun to use social networking services (SNSs) with their own devices, such as a desktop computer or smartphone. They frequently share knowledge and information for various purposes, and the number of those who use Internet content has become larger than ever.

In a network, content is transmitted using packets as a unit of transmission; these packets are delivered to their destinations by a router at the center of network. Since the router is a key device for interconnecting networks, it can acquire many kinds of information that are included in every packet stream. In fact, any packet can be passively captured by a router. A conventional router is a device that only forwards data packets between computer networks. When a data packet arrives, the router checks the address information in the packet header to determine its ultimate destination and directs the packet to the next network.

However, network traffic is growing year after year, and users have come to want even richer content. For example, at the Amazon online store, there is a recommendation service that collects users' purchase and browsing history and recommends goods related to this history according to an analysis. If we could analyze packet payloads on the routers, then we could create new services, not as infrastructure but as a service vendor.

We have proposed a new router, the Service-oriented Router (SoR) [1]. This router analyzes packets and can achieve content-based routing. SoR is not just routing hardware that transmits data and coverts protocols; it can analyze the semantic meaning of content, inspect traffic data streams including packet payloads, and provide functionalities in the application layer to servers, clients, and neighboring routers.

However, some packets in a network are encoded by the GZIP algorithm. In addition, in the Ethernet devices of a link layer, data that is larger than 1500 KB may be split into smaller packets. Many Internet users send or receive content to/from the network. These data are divided into packets and sent regardless of the order of the packets. In HTTP 1.1, which is generally used in Webpage access or Web data transfer, the GZIP compression option is available, and is used by some servers such as Amazon, Yahoo, Twitter, and The New York Times. Therefore, the SoR needs to decompress GZIP data for general packet analysis. This paper proposes a hardware GZIP decoder that can manage multiple data to adapt to content streams divided into packets. Using design architecture based on context switching, the proposed hardware can decode multiple users' data concurrently and effectively.

The remainder of this paper is organized as follows. Section II briefly introduces networks, SoR, and the GZIP algorithm. Section III explains related work. In Section IV, our proposed GZIP decoder hardware is explained. In Sections V and VI, we evaluated the architecture. Finally, Section VII concludes the paper.

2. Background

2.1 HTTP1.1, TCP/IP, ETHERNET

Most Internet throughput consists of HTTP packets, and the most widely used set of basic communications protocols is TCP/IP. The datagram is encapsulated by a TCP/IP header where some frame headers and footers are added to the original divided contents using Internet Protocol (IP). Figure 1 shows a brief overview of an Internet connection. IP is the principal communication protocol used for relaying packets over the Internet. It is responsible for forwarding packets by addressing hosts and routing datagrams from a source host to the destination host over one or more IP networks. Packets consist of two parts, IP headers and datagrams. The routing information required to route and deliver the datagram is included in the IP header.

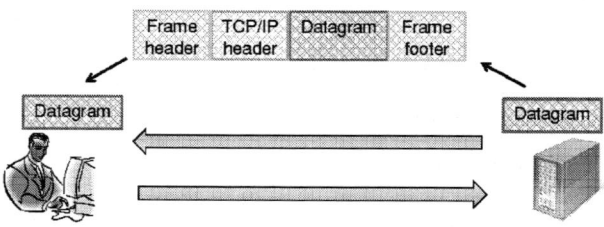

Fig. 1: Data Format

In HTTP1.1, the datagram is often compressed by GZIP [2],[3],[4], and then transmitted to a network. The need to send data via the Internet is growing, and many services are continuously provided to address this need. In order to send as much data as possible, a compression algorithm, generally GZIP, is used in HTTP1.1 protocols. The GZIP algorithm compresses data by 30-40% on average, and the size of data is reduced by more than half in most situations, enabling effective network utilization. Since GZIP is a free algorithm, anyone can use it, and it is widely used in the UNIX community.

2.2 Service-oriented Router (SoR)

Recently, Internet networking technologies have been significantly developed, and many individuals and commercial services now use these technologies. The Internet has become one of the most important infrastructures in our lives. Nowadays, people share knowledge and information for business and academic purposes over the Internet. It is now common for most people to use the Internet since it is very useful to send or receive information anytime, anywhere.

A network router is a device that connects several independent networks together and forwards data from source to destination. In order to manage lots of content, a new type of router is needed. Our laboratory has proposed a new router, called SoR, which can serve content-based services. General routers cannot provide these content-based services, and this implicitly limits the user experience and limits the benefits of a carrier. SoR provides services to end users from the router itself using a special application programming interface (API) based on SQL. It has many advantages because it enables passive data correction, which is different from

active data correction. In active data correction, end hosts can get required data only by accessing other hosts such as the Web crawlers of search engines. Current end-to-end systems have to correct data actively. This takes time, and the coverage of data correction is limited. Frequent crawling to obtain the real-time status of the Internet sometimes causes network congestion. Passive data correction of SoR enables real-time data acquisition and provides current Internet status without any network accesses.

For the SoR to analyze and correct data, a GZIP decoder is needed because packets may be encoded by an HTTP 1.1 GZIP algorithm at the end host server. In addition, there are various kinds of data on the Internet. SoR cannot decode perfectly without context management information, such as the streaming ID. Moreover, the network throughput has been increasing recently, and SoR will need to deal with throughput that is 10 Gbps or higher. A hardware GZIP decoder could be suitable for decoding multiple data quickly and concurrently.

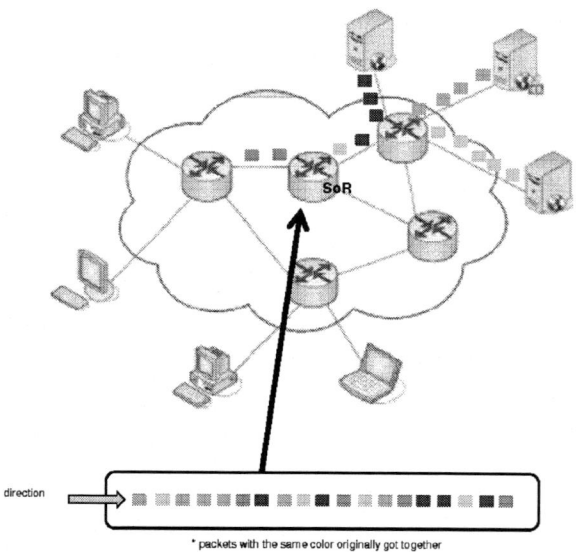

Fig. 2: Service-oriented Router

2.3 GZIP algorithm

In HTTP 1.1, transmitting compressed data is allowed, and the GZIP compression algorithm is used mainly in current network. GZIP is based on a deflate algorithm which consists of the Huffman [5] and LZ77 [6] algorithms. The header of compressed data has information such as the dictionary of the decoding process, which contains the rules to decode Huffman compressed binaries into ASCII codes. The dictionary, which is created at compression, is also used at decompression. Since LZ77 uses a sliding buffer up to 32 KB in size to compress and decompress iteration parts, a GZIP decoder must provide buffers of that size in the architecture.

Since each stream has independent dictionary information, the decoder hardware must create a dictionary table whenever a new stream arrives at the decoder. In addition, whenever a new packet arrives, the decoder needs to appropriately choose the dictionary information with the correct decoding rule for the packet.

3. Related Works

Few researchers work on Hardware GZIP decompression, probably because it has not been necessary to decompress GZIP encoded texts at network wire-speed before. There are three papers we are aware of that deal with hardware GZIP decoders. [7] and [8] implemented a GZIP decoder on FPGA and evaluated some values, such as the size of logic cells. However, they did not evaluate throughput, which is important for network analysis. Although [9] evaluates their throughput, it did not show other results, such as circuit area or number of logic cells used. This status makes it difficult for us to precisely compare these methods with our proposed method.

The research in [10] tackles the GZIP decoding problem with CPU and hardware collaboration. In this study, they implemented various kinds of compression methods in embedded systems. Though they implemented GZIP compression and decompression using hardware, they used the same Huffman dictionary generated during compression when decoding. In other words, their decoding hardware used the Huffman trees created by the compression process beforehand.

In addition, the studies described above do not deal with network traffic, in which data are separated into multiple packets. Reconstruction of all network streams from separated packets exhausts memory resources. This is the reason why context-switching technology is indispensable. The main papers that deal with compressed HTTP traffic are [11], [12], and [13]. The authors of these papers solve HTTP decompression using software implemented on gateway servers. These approaches are similar to our approach, and many good features are proposed to solve GZIP decompression. However, a software solution is limited in both throughput and the resources needed when used in an Internet router. Hence, these methods are not appropriate for our purpose. The proposed architecture is different from other studies in that it uses effective parallelizing architecture and on-the-fly analysis of HTTP traffic.

4. Implementation

In order to attain the wire-speed throughput of a network, we propose the following architecture for a hardware-based, parallel GZIP decoder for HTTP traffic, as shown in Figure 3. The proposed architecture consists of two main modules and various sub modules. One main module is a dictionary module that generates the dictionary from the header part of the GZIP encoded text. The other main module is the decoding module. The sub modules consist of input buffer modules and a switching module. The number of input buffers is the same as the total number of dictionary generation modules and decoding modules. These modules have a queue of registers that stores several input packets.

The proposed architecture has two main contributions: context switching and parallelizing. Context-switching technology enables the intermediate status of a GZIP decoding stream to be exchanged between the decoding modules and context buffers. The correct context, re-coded in a context buffer RAM, is selected and used by the decoding modules. Whenever a certain packet arrives and is buffered in a queue, the control logic fetches the correct context of the stream from the context buffer in which the packet belongs.

The proposed architecture decodes GZIP in two separate phases: a process in a dictionary generation module and a process in a decoding module. In this way, dictionary generation modules and decoding modules can work independently and in a parallel manner. While the dictionary generation module makes a dictionary for a certain stream, decoding modules concurrently decode other packets. This improves the throughput of the entire GZIP decoding process and this architecture allows the number of modules to be flexibly tuned according to the specifications of the target network throughput.

Using this context-switching design paradigm, the proposed hardware successfully continues decoding constantly, switching the intermediate status of one process after another according to the incoming network traffic. The number of contexts that can be handled at one time is approximately 10^5 in captured network traffic (Table 1). In this case, the size of the context memory needed is approximately 840 MB. This size is small enough to implement using an off-chip SRAM.

Table 1: an Average number of GZIP Streams.

timeout(s)	Number of GZIP streams
600	1.40×10^5
300	7.00×10^4
60	2.63×10^4
10	5.25×10^3

5. Evaluation

5.1 Environment

We evaluated the proposed GZIP decoding process using both ASIC and FPGA designs from the viewpoints of throughput and circuit area, or used slices. In this section, we evaluate the scale of the circuit and the throughput of the proposed decoding module. The decoding module

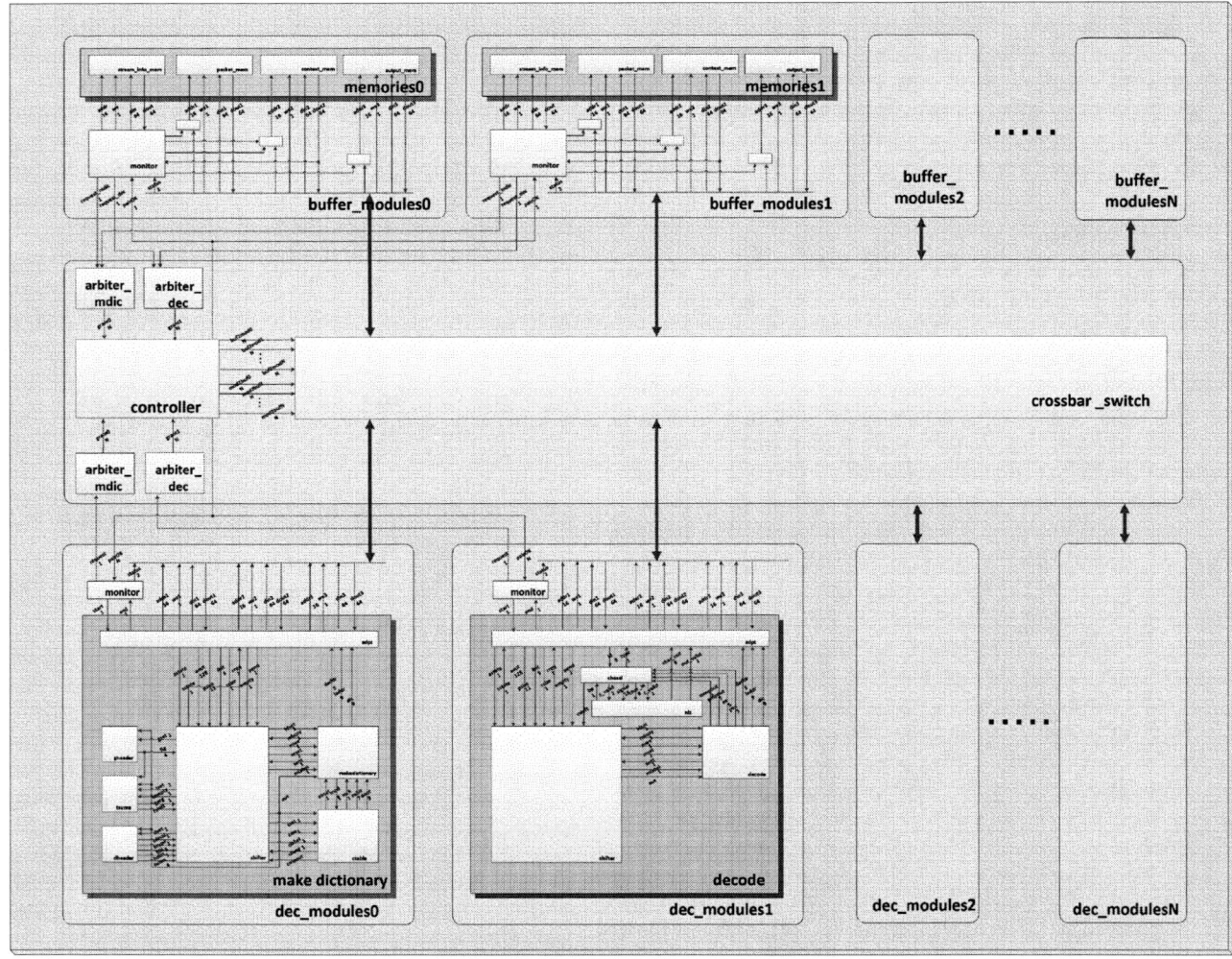

Fig. 3: Whole GZIP Decoding Architecture.

was implemented in Verilog HDL and synthesized using Xilinx ISE Design Suite 14.2 on an FPGA device (Vertex5 XC5VLX330T). For comparison, we used Synopsys Design Compiler 2005.09 by FREEPDK 45-nm Technology as the ASIC implementation.

First, we conducted an evaluation of real network traffic data to investigate its characteristics. In this data, the average size of one stream is 6,107 B, and it consists of 5 packets on average. We used HTTP traffic captured in our laboratory from 5 December 2011 to 13 December 2011. It includes approximately 0.5% GZIP encoded data.

Table 2 shows the evaluation environment of the proposed GZIP decoding module. Table 3 shows characteristics of the traffic data captured in Nishi Laboratory, which was used in this evaluation.

Table 2: an Environment of Simulation and Synthesis.

Language	Verilog-HDL
Logic Simulation	Cadence NC-Verilog LDV5.7
Wave Form tool	Cadence Simvision
ASIC synthesis tool	Synopsys Design Compiler X-2005.09
Library for ASIC synthesis	FreePDK OSU Library[14] (NAND2 gate area: 0.798 μm^2)

Table 3: Traffic Data in Nishi Laboratory for Evaluation.

Proportion of HTTP all bytes in the whole traffic	78%
Proportion of GZIP all bytes in the whole HTTP stream	7.05%
Proportion of GZIP all bytes in the whole stream	5.50%
Average packet size	1,221.54byte
Average GZIP compression rate	32.33%
Average size of GZIP decoded packet	3,778.43byte
Average # of packets contained in one GZIP stream	5packet

We created test data from data that was captured from www.kantei.go.jp, the Website of the Prime Minister of Japan and his Cabinet. The data size is 6.5 KB, or 31.4 KB when decompressed. This size is almost the same as the average size of a network stream. The data is captured using 36 parallel accesses to the Website, and the sampled dataset includes 36 streams. This data is stored into separate buffers. The number of buffers is equal to the total number of dictionary generation modules and decoding modules.

5.2 Performance

5.2.1 Waveforms in Simvision

In this research, we used the prepared test data from www.kantei.go.jp as described above. We analyzed the captured data, compressed the data with GZIP for testing, and conducted a simulation. Figure 4 shows the output waveform of the proposed hardware decoder.

5.2.2 ASIC evaluation

Figure 5 shows that the processing throughput increases to some extent as the number of decoding modules increases. Though the increase of decoding modules improves the total throughput, this is not always true if the number of modules exceeds eight. The throughput of the proposed decoder is 10.41 Gbps in the ASIC implementation, and the circuit area of the hardware is $0.14mm^2$. If we assume that there are 2.63×10^4 streams in a network, then the system needs 840 MB memory for managing context.

When the ratio of dictionary generation modules to decoding modules reaches 1:8, their throughput is almost equal. For instance, if the number of dictionary generation modules is 2, then 16 decoding modules achieves the best results for throughput. In other words, the optimum number of decoding module is influenced by the number of dictionary generation modules.

Figure 6 describes the index of throughput per circuit area for various numbers of modules. Using this index, we can compare different hardware configurations simultaneously. It reveals that the best performance is achieved when the number of dictionary generation modules is one and the number of decoding modules is eight. As the number of dictionary generation modules is increased, the performance decreases gradually because the dictionary module cannot be used fully, causing this index to deteriorate. In this evaluation, the result is almost the same as the evaluation of total throughput described in Figure 5.

5.2.3 FPGA evaluation

Table IV shows the throughput when the proposed architecture is implemented in FPGA using one dictionary generation module and eight decoding modules. For this evaluation, we implemented the proposed hardware in Virtex-5. The usage of register slices is approximately 13% whereas the usage of look-up-table slices is 29%. The usage of bock RAM is 40%. There are enough unused slices for implementing additional functions in the future.

Table 4: FPGA Synthesis and Simulation Result.

Minimum period	21.14ns
Minimum Frequency	47.30MHz
Throughput	0.71Gbps
Number of Slice Registers	13%
Number of Slice LUTs	29%
Number of fully used LUT-FF pairs	14%
Number of bounded IOBs	0%
Number of Block RAM	40%
Number of BUFG	9%

6. Discussion

The proposed system attains the best performance when GZIP decoding hardware is configured such that the ratio of dictionary generation modules to decoding modules is 1:8. This is because this ratio matches the existing ratio of GZIP dictionary headers to GZIP data in network traffic. This rate depends on the characteristics of the network traffic. Given the conditions of the captured traffic, it is effective to extend the hardware in keeping with the basic ratio, for instance, using 2 dictionary modules to 16 decoder modules, if the processing throughput needs to be improved in order to decode higher-throughput network traffic.

From another viewpoint, the circuit area of a dictionary generation module is approximately 3.5 times larger than that of a decoding module. Thus, it can be said that using fewer dictionary generation modules attains relatively better performance. A dictionary generation module generates approximately eight dictionaries whereas a decoding module decodes a single stream (five packets on average). In other words, dictionary generation modules and decoding modules constantly work together when their ratio is 1:8. Figure 7 shows the results when different ratios of modules are implemented. For the ratio of 1:8, indicated by the sky-blue waveforms of Figure 7, there are few blanks in both the dictionary generation and decoding processes. In the waveforms of ratios higher than 1:8, the dictionary generation module does not work constantly, though the decoding modules work relatively constantly. In contrast, below a ratio of 1:8, the decoding module waveform includes blank spaces caused by the decoder module waiting for the dictionary module. In these cases, the total latency of processing is almost same even for different ratios. This is caused by the waiting. Namely, there is a saturation point for the proposed hardware that depends on the characteristics of the Internet HTTP traffic.

7. Conclusions

This paper proposed hardware-based GZIP decoder modules for implementation in a SoR. In the evaluation, the

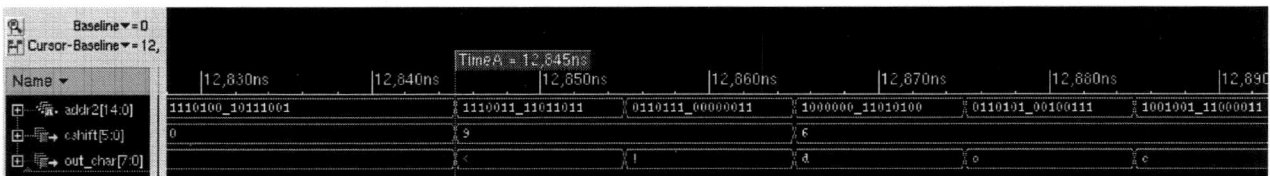

Fig. 4: Waveform of the Decoding.

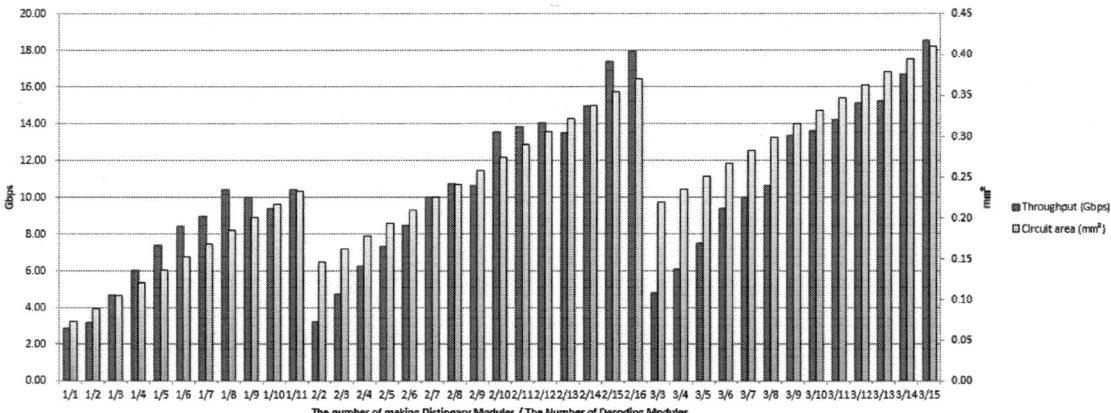

Fig. 5: Throughput and Circuit area of the Decoding in ASIC with the number of modules changed.

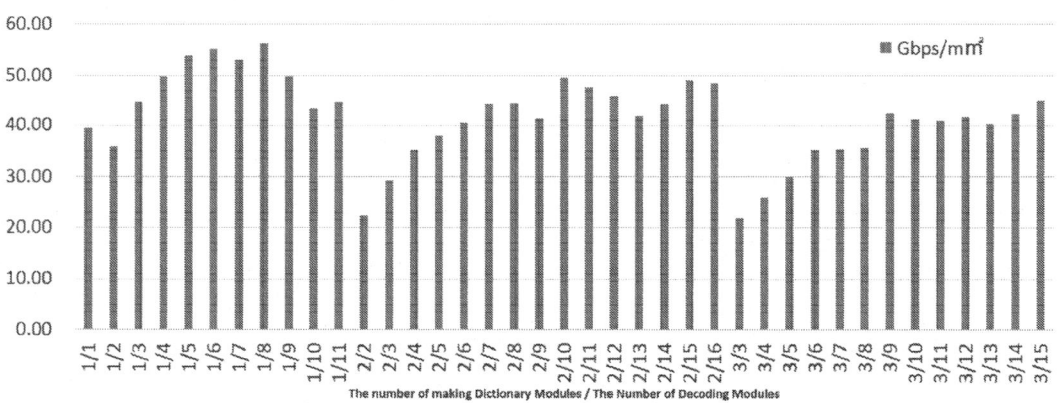

Fig. 6: Throughput per Circuit Area in ASIC with the number of modules changed.

number of decoding modules was varied, and the parallel utilization of GZIP decoder was evaluated. Since the simulation was conducted based on not software but hardware, the decoder could quickly manage the significant amount of GZIP data streaming on the Internet, and the use of context switching enabled concurrent decoding of multiple data streams. GZIP decoding hardware was evaluated using Verilog-HDL. When one dictionary generation module and eight decoding modules are used, the best throughput is achieved, 10.41 Gbps for an ASIC design and 0.71 Gbps for an FPGA design. The circuit area of that architecture is $0.14mm^2$.

8. Acknowledgment

This work was partially supported by Funds for the Integrated Promotion of Social System Reform and Research and Development, Ministry of the Environment and Grant-in-Aid for Scientific Research (B) (25280033). This work was also supported by VLSI Design and Education Center (VDEC), the University of Tokyo in collaboration with Synopsys, Inc., and Cadence Design Systems, Inc.

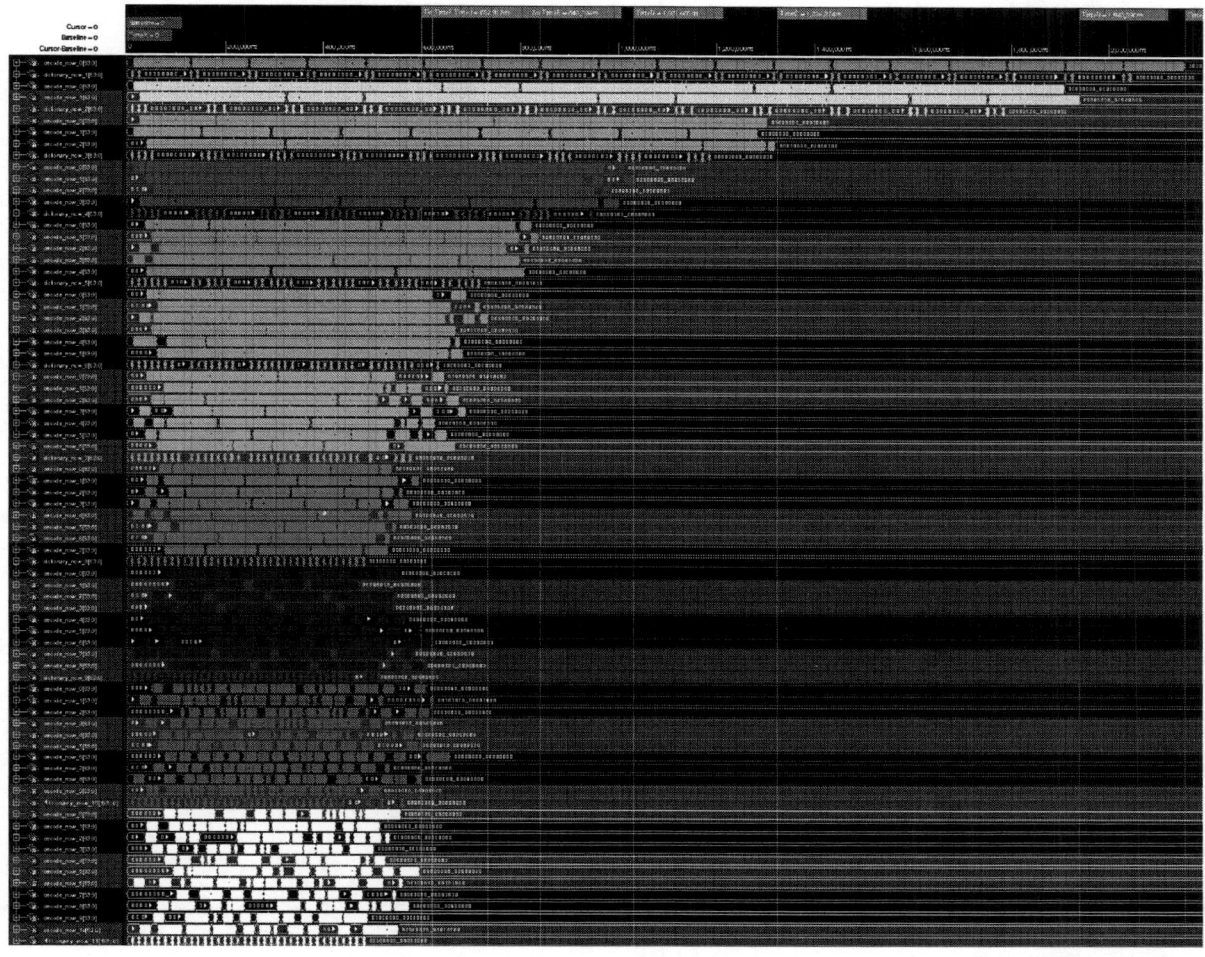

Fig. 7: Time Chart of the Simulation with Various Numbers of Modules. Each color line has a dictionary generation module (the lines below), and various numbers of decoding modules (the lines above).

References

[1] M. Koibuchi H. Kawashima K. Inoue, D. Akashi and H. Nish. Semantic router using data stream to enrich services. In *3rd International Conference on Future Internet CFI 2008 Seoul*, pp. 20–23, June 2008.

[2] P. Deutsch. Hypertext transfer protocol – http/1.1. `http://http://www.w3.org/Protocols/rfc2616/rfc2616-sec14.html#sec14.3`, June 1999.

[3] P. Deutsch. Deflate compressed data format specification version 1.3, May 1996. `http://www.ietf.org/rfc/rfc1951.txt`.

[4] P. Deutsch. Gzip file format specification version 4.3, May 1996. `http://www.ietf.org/rfc/rfc1952.txt`.

[5] D. Huffman. A method for the construction of minimum-redundancy codes. *Proc. IRE*, Vol. 40, No. 9, pp. 1098–1101, September 1952.

[6] J. Ziv and A. Lempel. A universal algorithm for sequential data compression. *IEEE Trans. Inf. Theory*, Vol. IT-23, No. 3, pp. 337–343, May 1977.

[7] S. Rigler, W. Bishop, and A. Kennings. Fpga-based lossless data compression using huffman and lz77 algorithms. In *Electrical and Computer Engineering, 2007. CCECE 2007. Canadian Conference on*, pp. 1235 –1238, april 2007.

[8] L. Perroton M. Akil and T. Grandpierre. FPGA-based architecture for hardware compression/decompression of wide format images. *Journal of Real-Time Image Processing*, Vol. 1, No. 2, pp. 163–170, September 2006.

[9] H. Luo J. Ouyang, C. Liu Z. Wang, J. Tian, and K. Sheng. FPGA implementation of GZIP compression and decompression for IDC services. *2010 International Conference on Field-Programmable Technology*, pp. 265–268, December 2010.

[10] C. Beckhoff D. Koch and J. Teich. Hardware decompression techniques for FPGA-based embedded systems. *Reconfigurable Technology and Systems*, Vol. 2, No. 2, pp. 1–23, 2009.

[11] A. Bremler-Barr and Y. Koral. Accelerating Multi-Patterns Matching on Compressed HTTP Traffic. *IEEE INFOCOM 2009 - The 28th Conference on Computer Communications*, pp. 397–405, April 2009.

[12] A. Bremler-Barr and Y. Koral. Accelerating Multipattern Matching on Compressed HTTP Traffic. *IEEE/ACM Transactions on Networking*, Vol. 20, No. 3, pp. 970–983, June 2012.

[13] A. Bremler-Barr Y. Afek and Y. Koral. Space efficient deep packet inspection of compressed web traffic. *Computer Communications*, Vol. 35, No. 7, pp. 810–819, April 2012.

[14] Freepdk. `http://www.eda.ncsu.edu/wiki/FreePDK`.

Simplifying Microblaze to Hermes NoC Communication through Generic Wrapper

Andres Benavides A.[1], Byron Buitrago P.[2], Johnny Aguirre M.[1]

[1] Electronic Engineering Department, University of Antioquia, Colombia

[2] Systems Engineering Department, University of Antioquia, Colombia

Abstract—In this paper an easy microprocessor to NoC connection strategy, based in a hardware wrapper design is proposed. The implemented wrapper simplifies the connection between a network on chip infrastructure and several MicroBlaze softcore processors. Proposed strategy improves the design process of a parallel computing environment. Wrapper development process, synthesis results and functionality test are showed and analyzed.

Key words: FPGA, Multicore, Hermes NoC, MicroBlaze, FSL bus, Embedded processors.

1. INTRODUCTION

Nowadays, computer applications need more than one processor to resolve complex tasks in short time. This particular fact has generated a new tendency in the design of high performance electronic systems. In an effort to improve the performance of a single processor scheme, multiprocessor architectures have been proposed. A multiprocessor (or multi-core) system takes advantage of the billion transistor era to achieve high performance by running multiple tasks simultaneously, on independent processors, decreasing applications execution time. However, parallel processing faces a lot of troubles, among which may be mentioned: Shared memory access and communication infrastructure. In a multi-core system, efficient communication among CPUs is a critical item to performance measurement. In reduced multi-core systems, a common bus is enough to connect the components. However with more than 8 cores a bus is not scalable because bus electrical load increases while its speed is reduced, and the bandwidth demand is not satisfied [1].

A scalable and efficient solution to connect on-chip components is a packet-switched on-chip network (NoC) [2]. Network-on-Chip (NoC) brings the techniques developed for macro-scale, multi-hop networks into a chip. Hermes [3], AET [4], Xpipes [5], are examples of NoC's implementation. By means of NoC, systems communications improve by modularity support, cores reuse, and scalability increase. Those features enable a higher level of abstraction in multicore's architectural modeling and allow heterogeneous systems building.

Another big problem in multicore architectures is related to quick prototyping capability. Traditionally, it has been only possible put under test the system once the silicon is available. In last years, softcore implementation on FPGA has emerged as a solution to rapid prototyping, due to their reduced cost, flexibility, platform independence and greater immunity to obsolescence [6]. A soft-core processor is a hardware description language (HDL) model of a specific processor (CPU) which can be customized for specific application requirements and synthesized for an ASIC or FPGA target. Examples of softcore are OpenRisc 1200 [7], LEON [8] and MicroBlaze [9]. Several architectures based in softcores can be found on internet sites as OpenCores [10] or Xilinx [11]. However typically softcore designs are limited to single processor or reduce multi-processors architectures connected by shared bus structure.

In this paper a strategy based in a hardware wrapper to simplify the connection between the Hermes NoC and MicroBlaze processor in order to facilitate the multicore architecture prototyping and design is proposed.

This paper starts with a background section in order to understand Hermes network on chip and MicroBlaze architecture. Then, wrapper design and internal architecture are explained. Wrapper implementation results, functionality test, conclusions and future work are showed and discussed at the end of this paper.

2. PRELIMINARIES AND BACKGROUND INFORMATION

2.1. NOC INFRASTRUCTURE

We have employed as communication infrastructure the HERMES NoC, developed by Moraes et al. [3]. The NoC (Figure 1) is formed by IP blocks and routers which are connected on a mesh topology. In Moraes' NoC each IP block represents a computational element; in our case an IP block means MicroBlaze (MB) CPU. A unique address is associated to each router on the net. The IP blocks have the same router's address to which they are connected.

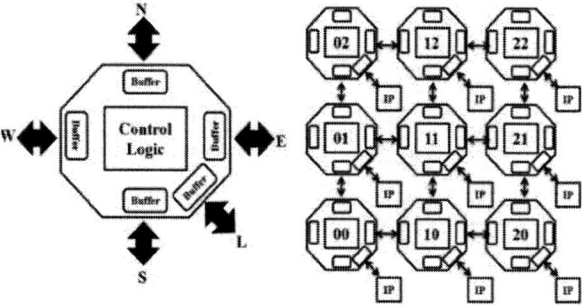

Figure 1. Router and a 3×3 HERMES NoC

All IP blocks can communicate with each other by sending packets on a rate of 500Mbps by each router. A valid packet is formed by a set of flits (1flit=8bits) according the formats illustrate in the Figure 2. Hermes NoC uses the wormhole flow-control for packet transference and a bi-dimensional routing algorithm.

	1st flit	2nd flit	3rd flit	4th flit	5th flit	6th flit	7th flit	8th flit
Read	Target Address	Payload Size 4	Source Address	Code 0	Address [15:8]	Address [7:0]		
Write	Target Address	Payload Size 6	Source Address	Code 1	Address [15:8]	Address [7:0]	Data [15:8]	Data [7:0]
Start Stop	Target Address	Payload Size 2	Source Address	Code 2				
Return Read	Target Address	Payload Size 4	Source Address	Code 9	Data [15:8]	Data [7:0]		

Figure 2. HERMES NoC packet's formats

The router transfers packets among IP blocks by means of 4 bidirectional ports (North, South, East and West), and a local port (to connect an IP block). The Figure 3 shows physical connection between two consecutive ports. Each port has an output and input gates. Each one of them has a FIFO memory buffer to temporal information storage. In the output gate, the *tx* indicates that there is a flit in the *data_out* bus, the signal is cancelled when the *ack_tx* signal is received. In the input gate the *rx* signal indicates that there is a flit in the *data_in* bus, when it is taken and sent to other router (or to the IP block), the *ack_rx* signal is generated.

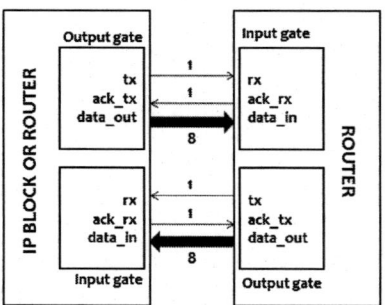

Figure 3. Example of Router's port

Any IP block can be plugged into the network once it is equipped with the proper interface (wrapper). The wrapper adapts the IP block to router connection signals. The sections 3 explain how MicroBlaze processors were connected into the Hermes NoC.

2.2. MICROBLAZE SOFTCORE

The MicroBlaze core (Figure 5) is organized as Harvard architecture with separate bus interface units for data and instruction accesses. Each bus interface unit is further split into a Local Memory Bus (LMB) and IBM's On-chip Peripheral Bus (OPB). Further, MicroBlaze core provides 8 input and 8 output interfaces to Fast Simplex Link (FSL) buses. The FSL buses are unidirectional, non-arbitrated, dedicated and synchronized communication channels. The FSL bus transmits data directly from the MicroBlaze core to other peripherals or processors buses in master-slave scheme without using a shared bus. MicroBlaze contains several instructions to read from the input FSLs and write to the output FSLs. Each read and write operations consume two FPGA's clock cycles.

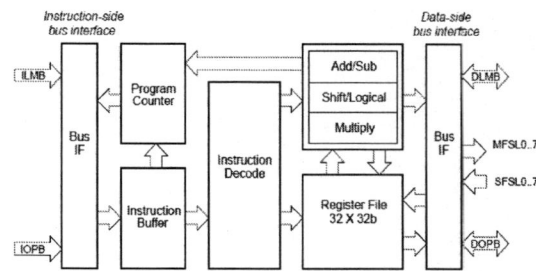

Figure 4. MicroBlaze Core Block Diagram

We have employed the FSL bus to connect the MicroBlaze to designed wrapper due its high speed communication. The FLS signals are showed in the Figure 4.

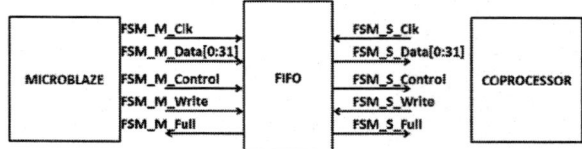

Figure 4. MicroBlaze Core Block Diagram

A FIFO memory buffer is used as interface between the Microblaze and the other peripheral. Buffer allows using different clock sources for the *FSL_M_Clk* and *FSL_S_Clk* signals. In a master to slave writing process the master checks the *FSL_M_Full* signal to known the FIFO state. When the FIFO is available (*FSL_M_Full*=0) the master puts the data on the *FSL_M_data* bus and activates the *FSL_M_Write* signal. On the slave side the signal *FSL_S_Exists* indicates it that a data should be read. The peripheral takes the data by means the *FSL_S_Data* bus and activates the *FSL_S_Read* signal as acknowledge.

The optional *FSL_M_Control* and *FSL_S_Control* signals can be used to coordinate the communication. In a slave to master writing process the roles between the Microblaze and the peripheral are inverted. Also, the FIFO depth can be increased to raise the performance communication.

3. FSL WRAPPER ARCHITECTURE

The designed wrapper allows to plug each processor with the NoC infrastructure [12]. The wrapper takes the signals from FSL and translates them to router´s properly signals. In this way, wrapper functionality can be interpreted how FSL to NoC and NoC to FSL communications abstraction layer. In the first case, flits arrive from FSL to be routed by the NoC. In the second case, flits arrive from NoC to be sent to the MicroBlaze.

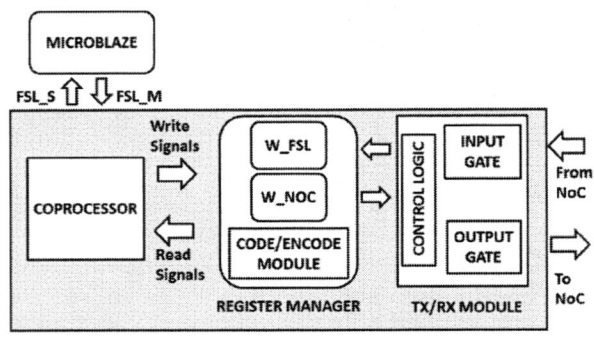

Figure 5. FSL to NoC wrapper

The wrapper (Figure 5) is composed by a coprocessor, a register manager and Tx/Rx Module.

- Coprocessor: It takes the FSL signals described in the section 2, and generates asynchronous signals to write or read in the register manager.
- Register Manager: In the FSL to NoC communication process, it receives the frames sent by the coprocessor, decodes and saves them in the *W-FSL* register. In the NoC to FSL communication process, it takes the data from *W-NoC* register, encodes and sends them to coprocessor.
- Tx/Rx Module: It fixes the connection with the router's local port. Input and output gates, described at section 2, are its main components. This module takes flits from *W-FSL* register and puts them on the output gate. In the other way, it takes the data from the input gate and writes them on the *W-NoC* register in the manager register module.

Packets' integrity is guaranteed by NoC infrastructure. However it was necessary to implement a local protocol for wrapper in order to ensure the correct communication between MicroBlaze and router. In this local protocol, each packet is transmitted in three frames according the format

shown in figure 6. The control field indicates which frame is been sending. The decode module in the register manager interpreters those frames. When one field is lost, the whole frame is rebroadcast.

	Control	1st Flit	2nd Flit	3th flit
1st Frame	0x01	Target Address	Payload Size	Code
2nd Frame	0x02	Address [15:8]	Address [7:0]	0x02
3th Frame	0x03	Data [15:8]	Data [7:0]	0x03

Figure 6. Wrapper protocol

The wrapper also allows to see NoC like an extension of the FSL bus. Therefore, NoC's writing and reading tasks can be managed using high level functions available for the FSL since a programming language. The example 1 shows the C function to send a packet from MicroBlaze to NoC.

```
void writeNoc(char tg, char sz, char cm,
        char adH, char adL, char daH,char daL)
{
    auxTx = 0x01<<24 | tg<<16 | sz<<8 | cm;
    putfsl(auxTx, FSL_MASTER);

    auxTx = 0x02<<24 | adH<<16 | adL<<8 |0x02;
    putfsl(auxTx, FSL_MASTER);

    auxTx = 0x03<<24 | daH<<16 | daL<<8 |0x03;
    putfsl(auxTx, FSL_MASTER);

}
```

Example 1. FSL to NoC writing process

The example 2 shows the function to read a packet from NoC.

```
void readNoc (char * frame)
{
    getfsl(auxRx,FSL_SLAVE);
    frame->tg=(char)(auxRx>>16);
    frame->sz=(char)(auxRx>>8);
    frame->cm=(char)auxRx;

    getfsl(auxRx,FSL_SLAVE);
    frame->adH=(char)(auxRx>>16);
    frame->adL=(char)(auxRx>>8);

    getfsl(auxRx,FSL_SLAVE);
    frame->daH=(char)(auxRx>>16);
    frame->daL=(char)(auxRx>>8);
}
```

Example 2. NoC to FSL reading process

4. WRAPPER TEST

To study the wrapper functionality, it was generated an architecture with three MicroBlaze CPUs connected through the designed wrapper to Hermes NoC. A serial port was included for debug purposes. The whole system is illustrated in the figure 7.

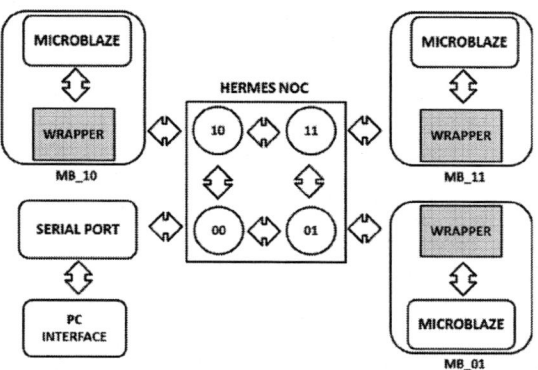

Figure 7. Study case architecture.

EDK Xilinx tool was used to generate each MicroBlaze core. The SDK Xilinx's tool was employed to generate the software. Individual programs were written by each processor. Stop y Start commands ensures the coordination of communication processes. Finally ISE tool was used to make the connection among MicroBlaze processors, designed wrappers and NoC infrastructure. The whole system was synthetized on the Virtex 4 FX20 FPGA. The synthesis report is illustrated on the table 1.

MODULE	Power(W)		LUTs	Signals
	Dynamic	Quiescent		
MB	0,183	0,256	2610	3006
WR	0.013	0.219	71	148
MB+WR	0,189	0,256	2891	3374
SERIAL	0.020	0.219	321	374
NOC	0.038	0.220	1912	2178
WHOLE	0.651	0.324	7490	10189

Table 1. Synthesis report.

The figure 8 shows application running results, data was taken from a serial port sniffer. It shows a token passing example, where each MicroBlaze takes a common variable, increases it and passes to the next MicroBlaze and a serial port.

The string *"Print from MicroBlaze 01, i=1"*, is a message sent by processor 01 in the net. *"Print from MicroBlaze 10, i=2"*, is a message sent by 10 in the net and *"Print from MicroBlaze 11, i=3"*, is a message sent by processor 11 in the net. The serial interface has 00 coordinate in the net.

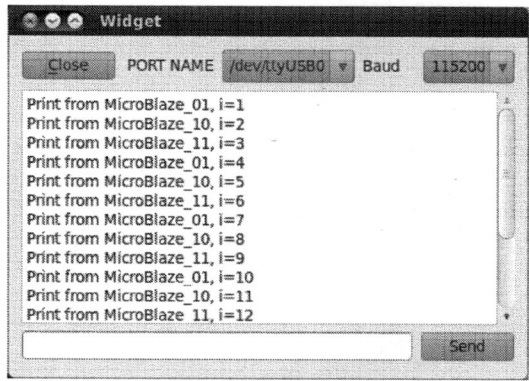

Figure 8. Application.

5. CONCLUSIONS AND FUTURE IDEAS

In this paper a hardware wrapper to simplify the multicore architecture design and prototyping, using the Hermes NoC and the MicroBlaze softcore was introduced. The wrapper test showed the low cell units occupied the functionality and the good performance of the proposed wrapper.

FSL employment to connect the MicroBlaze with NoC allows to give to the developer a higher abstraction level, through simple software language functions calls hidden low level details.

On the other hand, the network structure ensures the scalability and enables a multicore architecture can be built in a modular way. This scheme reduces design time because it allows a considerable components reusing strategy.

The reconfigurable hardware environment allows architectural customization. This feature enables heterogeneous design, particularly in Virtex FPGA, PowerPC CPU can be employed in our multicore system using Hermes NoC due with developed wrapper, without the necessity of any change.

Future ideas cover applications design using multicore platform. Those applications involve signal processing, simultaneous multisensory acquisitions, scientific computations, server clusters, hardware accelerators among others.

6. ACKNOWLEDGMENTS

The authors would thank to Microelectronics and Control group of University of Antioquia, who provided the software and hardware tools during project realization.

REFERENCES

[1] G. Nychis, C. Fallin, T. Moscibroda, O Mutlu. "Next Generation On-Chip Networks: What Kind of Congestion Control Do We Need," Hotnets-IX Proceedings of the 9th ACM SIGCOMM Workshop on Hot Topics in Network, October 20–21, 2010.

[2] L. Benini and G. de Micheli, "Networks on Chips: A New SoC Paradigm," IEEE Computer, Jan. 2002.

[3] Fernando Moraes, Ney Calazans, Aline Mello, Leandro Möller, Luciano Ost: "HERMES: an infrastructure for low area overhead

packet-switching networks on chip", the VLSI Journal, vol. 38-1, 2004.

[4]   T. Valtonen et al., "An autonomous error-tolerant cell for scalable network-on-chip architectures," in Norchip, Nov. 2001, pp. 198–203.

[5]   D. Bertozzi et al., "NoC synthesis flow for customized domain specific multiprocessor systems-on-chip," IEEE Trans. Parallel and Distributed Systems,vol. 16, no. 2, pp. 113–129, Feb. 2005.

[6]   Jason G. Tong, Ian D. L. Anderson and Mohammed A. S. Khalid, "Soft-Core Processors for Embedded Systems," The 18th International Confernece on Microelectronics (ICM) 2006.

[7]   D. Lampret. OpenRISC1200 IP Core specification. www.opencores.org.

[8]   Gaisler Research Website, www.gaisler.com, January 2013.

[9]   Xilinx, Inc. Xilinx Platform Studio and the Embedded Development Kit, EDK version 13.1 edition. www.xilinx.com/tools/platform.htm

[10] Opencores Website, www. http://opencores.org, January 2013.

[11] Xilins Website, http://www.xilinx.com, January 2013.

[12] Benavides, A.; Aedo, J.; Rivera, F., "Multi-purpose System-on-Chip platform for rapid prototyping," Circuits and Systems (LASCAS), 2012 IEEE Third Latin American Symposium on , vol., no., pp.1,4, Feb. 29 2012-March 2 2012.

An Area-Efficient Asynchronous FPGA Architecture for Handshake-Component-Based Design

Yoshiya Komatsu, Masanori Hariyama, and Michitaka Kameyama
Graduate School of Information Sciences, Tohoku University
Aoba 6-6-05, Aramaki, Aoba, Sendai, Miyagi, 980-8579, Japan

Abstract—*This paper presents an area-efficient FPGA architecture for handshake-component-based design. The handshake-component-based design is suitable for large-scale, complex asynchronous circuit because of its understandability. However, conventional FPGA architecture for handshake-component-based design is not area-efficient because of its complex logic blocks. This paper proposes an area-efficient FPGA architecture that combines complex logic blocks (LBs) and simple LBs. Complex LBs implement handshake components that implement data path controller, and simple LBs implement handshake component that implement data path. The FPGA based on the proposed architecture is implemented in a 65nm process. Its evaluation results show that the proposed FPGA can implement asynchronous circuits efficiently.*

Keywords: FPGA, Reconfigurable LSI, Self-timed circuit, Asynchronous circuit

1. Introduction

Field-programmable gate arrays (FPGAs) are widely used to implement special-purpose processors. FPGAs are cost-effective for small-lot production because functions and interconnections of logic resources can be directly programmed by end users. Despite their design cost advantage, FPGAs impose large power consumption overhead compared to custom silicon alternatives [1]. The overhead increases packaging costs and limits integrations of FPGAs into portable devices. In FPGAs, the power consumption of clock distribution is a serious problem because it has an enormously large number of registers than custom VLSIs. To cut the clock distribution power, some asynchronous FPGAs has been proposed [2], [3], [4], [5], [6]. However, the problem is that it is difficult to design asynchronous circuits and few CAD tools or design flow for asynchronous FPGAs have been introduced. To solve the problem, we proposed an FPGA architecture for handshake-component-based asynchronous circuit design (HCFPGA) [7]. In handshake-component-based design, asynchronous circuits are designed by connecting handshake components. Since various handshake components such as for data processing and data path control are defined, it is easy to design asynchronous data path and its controller. Besides, there are hardware description languages and circuit synthesis tools

for handshake-component-based design [8], [9]. Therefore, handshake-component-based design is suitable for complex large-scale asynchronous circuits. However, the problem of the previous HCFPGA is its large transistor count because each FPGA cell is complex to support various handshake components.

This paper proposes an area-efficient HCFPGA architecture that combines complex LBs and simple LBs. As the proposed architecture implements handshake components efficiently, CAD tools such as Balsa [9] are utilized to design asynchronous applications. Data path and its controller are implemented by simple LBs and complex LBs respectively. Therefore, the proposed architecture can implement applications efficiently.

2. Architecture

2.1 Handshake-component-based design methodology

In asynchronous circuits, the handshake protocol is used for synchronization instead of using the clock. Figure 1 shows a four-phase handshake sequence. First, active port sets the request wire to "1" as shown in Fig. 1(a). Second, passive port sets the acknowledge wire to "1" as shown in Fig. 1(b). Third, active port sets the request wire to "0" as shown in Fig. 1(c). Finally, passive sets the acknowledge wire to "0" as shown in Fig. 1(d) and wire values return to initial state. Data signals are sent along with request signals or acknowledge signals.

Handshake components were proposed for use in the synthesis of the language Tangram [8] created by Philips Research. An asynchronous functional element such as a binary operator is denoted by a handshake component. There are 46 handshake components [10] and each handshake component is used for data processing or data path control. Figure 2 shows handshake components. Handshake components constitute a handshake circuit. Figure 3 shows an example of a handshake circuit. Each handshake component has ports and is connected to another handshake component through a channel. Communication between handshake components is done by sending request signal from the "active" port and acknowledge signal from the "passive" port. Depending on the kind of handshake components, data signals are sent along with request signals or acknowledge signals. The number of

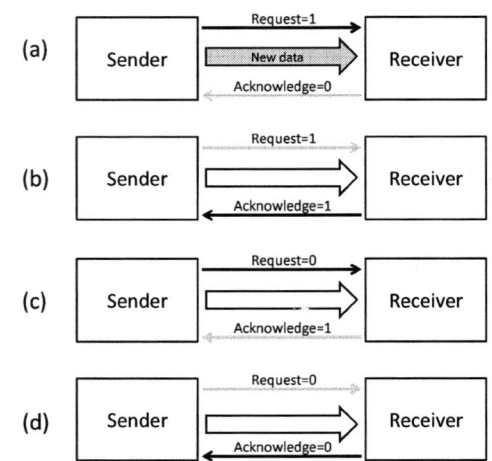

Fig. 1: A four-phase handshake sequence.

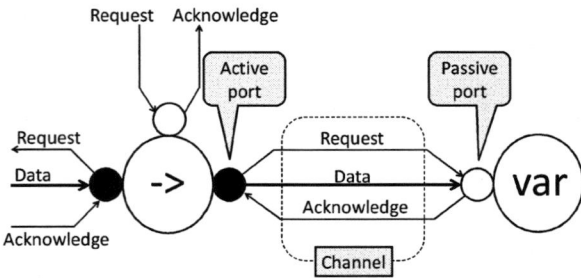

Fig. 2: Handshake components and channels.

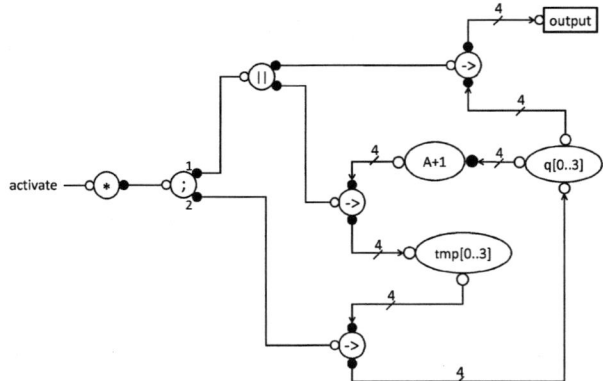

Fig. 3: A simple handshake circuit (4 bit counter).

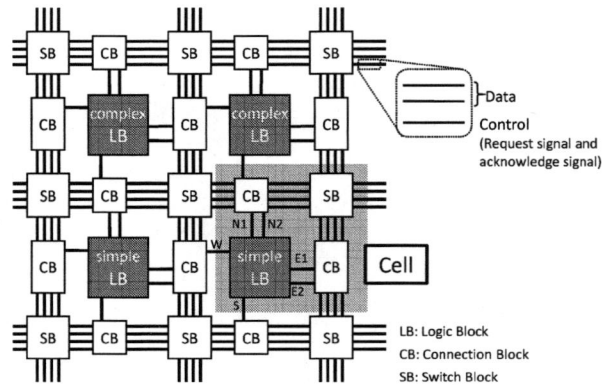

Fig. 4: Overall architecture.

ports of a handshake component and the width of data signal can be varied. Each handshake components execute complex handshake sequences through channels. However, handshake circuits are easily understandable and manageable because a function of each handshake component is clear and each handshake is symbolized by a channel and ports. Also, there are tools that translate high-level circuit description into handshake circuit to synthesize asynchronous circuit. Thus, handshake-component-based design is suitable for complex and large-scale asynchronous circuits. Asynchronous circuit synthesis is done by replacing each handshake component with corresponding circuit.

2.2 Overall architecture

As mentioned in preceding section, circuit synthesis is done by replacing each handshake component with corresponding circuit. Thus, asynchronous circuits can be implemented by replacing each handshake component with a combination of LBs. Figure 4 shows the overall architecture of the proposed FPGA. The FPGA consists of mesh-connected cells like conventional FPGAs. Each cell includes an LB, two Connection Blocks (CBs) and a Switch Block (SB). There are two types of LBs. One is complex LB and the other is

simple LB. The upper CB connects SBs to N1, N2 and S terminals of two LBs, and the bottom CB connects SBs to E1, E2 and W terminals. In the proposed architecture, each LB includes dedicated circuits for implementing handshake components. Therefore, the proposed architecture can implement handshake circuits efficiently. The proposed architecture can implement 39 out of 46 handshake components defined in Balsa manual [10]. Handshake components that have multiple ports or wide data path can be implemented using several LBs. In the proposed FPGA architecture, the Four-Phase Dual-Rail (FPDR) encoding is employed for asynchronous data encoding. The FPDR encoding encodes a bit and a request signal onto two wires. Table 1 shows the code table of the FPDR encoding. The main feature is that the sender sends a spacer and a valid data alternately as shown in Fig. 5. FPDR circuits are robust to the delay variation. Hence, the FPDR encoding is the ideal one for FPGAs in which the data path is programmable. Because the FPDR encoding is employed, three wires are required for a data bit. Two wires are used for the data encoded in FPDR encoding, and one wire for the acknowledge signal.

Table 1: Code table of the FPDR encoding.

	Code word (T, F)
Data 0	(0,1)
Data 1	(1,0)
Spacer	(0,0)

Fig. 5: Example of the FPDR encoding.

2.3 Logic block structure

As mentioned in 2.2, there are complex LB and simple LB. Figure 6 and 7 show the structures of a complex LB and simple LB. Complex LB consists of a BinaryFunction module, a Variable module, a Sequence module, a CallMUX module, a Case module, an Encode module, an Input switch box and an Output switch box. Simple LB consists of a BinaryFunction module, a Variable module, a C-element, an Input switch box and an Output switch box. An Input switch box and an Output switch box connect modules to CBs. Each module is used to implement a handshake component. Table 2 shows correspondence relation between modules and handshake components. Complex LB can supports 39 handshake components because it has all the modules. On the other hand, simple cell can implement 22 handshake components including Variable component and BinaryFunction component. Therefore, complex LB is suitable for implementing data path controller and simple LB can implement data path efficiently.

3. Evaluation

The proposed FPGA is implemented in e-Shuttle 65nm CMOS process with 1.2V supply. The circuits are evaluated using HSPICE simulation. Table 3 shows the comparison

Table 2: Handshake components and its corresponding resources.

Module	Handshake component
Variable	BuiltinVariable, Variable
Sequence	Concur, Loop, Sequence, While
CallMUX	Call, CallMUX, Continue, ContinuePush
Case	CallDEMUX, Case, CaseFetch, DecisionWait, PassivatorPush, SynchPush
Encode	Encode
BinaryFunction and Variable	BinaryFunc, BinaryFuncConstR, UnaryFunc
Variable and Sequence	FalseVariable, ActiveEagerFalseVariable, PassiveEagerFalseVariable
Programmable Interconnect resources	Adapt, Combine, CombineEqual, Constant, Fetch, Fork, ForkPush, Halt, HaltPush, Passivator, Slice, Split, SplitEqual, Synch, SynchPull, WireFork

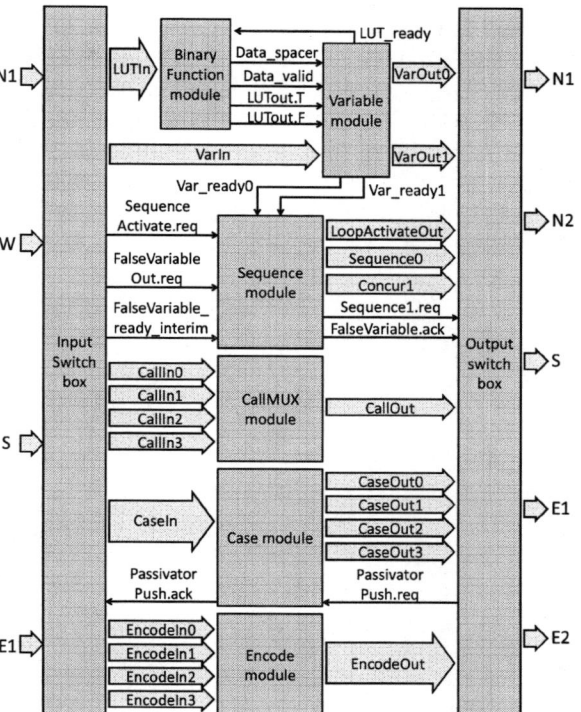

Fig. 6: Structure of a complex LB.

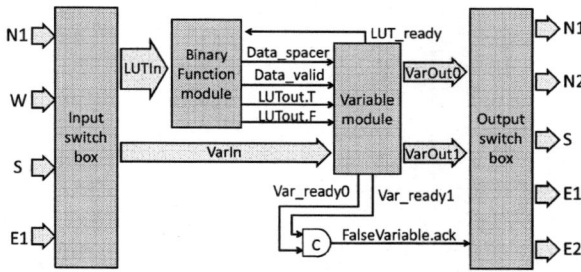

Fig. 7: Structure of a simple LB.

result of cells of the conventional asynchronous FPGA, the conventional HCFPGA and the proposed HCFPGA. Compared to the conventional asynchronous FPGA cell, the transistor count of the complex cell is increased by 63.0% because the complex cell is the same as the conventional HCFPGA cell. The transistor count of the simple cell is reduced by 31.0% compared to the complex cell.

The next evaluation shows the implementation results of a 4-bit counter. Table 4 shows the comparison of transistor counts, energy consumptions per operation and throughputs. Compared to the conventional asynchronous FPGA, the number of transistors and the energy consumption per operation are reduced by 4.4% and 19.8% respectively. This is because handshake-component-based design method is suitable for designing not only controllers but also area-efficient data paths. On the other hand, the throughput is decreased by 47.6% because each handshake components execute complex handshake sequence. Compared to the conventional HCFPGA, the number of transistors and the energy consumption per operation are reduced by 25.3% and 11.8% respectively and the throughput is increased by 7.9%. This is because the data path is implemented using the cells with simple LB.

Table 3: Transistor count of a cell and its breakdown.

	Conventional Asynchronous FPGA	Conventional HCFPGA	Proposed HCFPGA	
			Complex cell	Simple cell
Cell	2423	3949	3949	2726
LB	611	1311	1311	611
SB and CBs	1812	2638	2638	2115

Table 4: Evaluation results of 4-bit counter.

	Conventional Asynchronous FPGA	Conventional HCFPGA	Proposed HCFPGA
Number of transistors	33922	43439	32432
Energy Consumption [pJ]	5.14	4.68	4.13
Throughput [M operations/sec]	160.63	77.93	84.09

4. Conclusions

This paper presented an area-efficient asynchronous FPGA architecture for handshake-component-based design. In the proposed HCFPGA architecture, simple LB and complex LB are used to implement a data path and its controller respectively. Therefore, the proposed architecture implements applications efficiently. As a future work, we are evaluating the proposed FPGA architecture on some practical benchmarks.

Acknowledgment

This work is supported by VLSI Design and Education Center (VDEC), the University of Tokyo in collaboration with STARC, e-Shuttle, Inc., Fujitsu Ltd., Cadence Design Systems Inc. and Synopsys Inc.

References

[1] V. George H. Zhang. and J. Rabaey, "The design of a low energy FPGA," in *Proceedings of 1999 International Symposium on Low Power Electronics and Design*, California, USA, Aug 1999, pp. 188–193.

[2] J. Teifel and R. Manohar, "An asynchronous dataflow FPGA architecture," *IEEE Transactions on Computers*, vol. 53, no. 11, pp. 1376–1392, 2004.

[3] R. Manohar, "Reconfigurable Asynchronous Logic," in *Proceedings of IEEE Custom Integrated Circuits Conference*, Sep. 2006, pp. 13–20.

[4] M. Hariyama, S. Ishihara, and M. Kameyama, "Evaluation of a Field-Programmable VLSI Based on an Asynchronous Bit- Serial Architecture," *IEICE Trans. Electron*, vol. E91-C, no. 9, pp. 1419–1426, 2008.

[5] M. Hariyama, S. Ishihara, , and M. Kameyama, "A Low-Power Field-Programmable VLSI Based on a Fine-Grained Power-Gating Scheme," in *Proceedings of IEEE International Midwest Symposium on Circuits and Systems (MWSCAS)*, Knoxville(USA), Aug 2008, pp. 430–433.

[6] S. Ishihara, Y. Komatsu, M. Hariyama and M. Kameyama, "An Asynchronous Field-Programmable VLSI Using LEDR/4-Phase-Dual-Rail Protocol Converters," in *Proceedings of The International Conference on Engineering of Reconfigurable Systems and Algorithms (ERSA)*, Las Vegas(USA), Jul 2009, pp. 145–150.

[7] Y. Komatsu, M. Hariyama and M. Kameyama, "Architecture of an Asynchronous FPGA for Handshake-Component-Based Design," *Proc. International Conference on Engineering of Reconfigurable Systems and Algorithms (ERSA)*, pp. 133-136, July 2012

[8] K. van Berkel, J. Kessels, M. Roncken, R. Saeijs, and F. Schalij, " The VLSI-programming language Tangram and its translation into handshake circuits," in *Proc. EDAC*, 1991, pp. 384—389.

[9] A. Bardsley, "Implementing Balsa Handshake Circuits," Ph.D. thesis, Dept. of Computer Science, University of Manchester, 2000.

[10] Doug Edwards and Andrew Bardsley and Lilian Janin and Luis Plana and Will Toms, "Balsa: A Tutorial Guide", 2006.

Int'l Conf. Reconfigurable Systems and Algorithms | ERSA'13 |

19

Implementing 2x1 Transmit Diversity on Software Defined Radios

Anaam Ansari, *Graduate Student, San Jose State University*, Dr. Robert Morelos Zaragoza, *Professor, San Jose State University.*

Abstract— **The premise of this project is to provide a proof of concept of Alamouti's remarkably celebrated 2x1 transmit diversity scheme with the aid of Software Defined Radios. We aim at producing the same results as Alamouti, in an environment that behaves as a frequency selective and slow fading channel. The software-defined radios provide a remote RF front-end to conduct this experiment however; the real encoding and combining are done through Simulink natively on external host machines.**

Index Terms—Alamouti, DBPSK, Mathworks Simulink,Matched Filter, PN sequences,Space Time Encoding, Software Defined Radios, USRP2.

I. INTRODUCTION

Throughout the development of wireless communication systems, the environment poses an insurmountable challenge as our demands for mobility increase. With increased mobility, wireless channels become riddled with multipath and fading effects. Typically a communication system is highly susceptible to effects of multipath and fading unless it is compensated for additionally. Diversity is an elegant solution to this problem. Diversity is defined as the availability of more than one channel to transmit multiple copies of the same information. This kind of redundancy in a communication system is welcomed, since, it promises a better performance as opposed to a traditional setup that does not adopt diversity. Conventionally, diversity on the receiver side was observed for harvesting information with the help of more than one antenna. This kind of simultaneous reception of the same data through different antenna provides us with resourceful, redundant information. In an influential environment, data often loses its integrity and thus the redundant information helps us compensate for the channel influences and recover the data more precisely. Receiver diversity calls for increasing the RF circuitry such as low noise amplifiers (LNA) by two fold. In 1998, Siavash M. Alamouti proposed, that his novel idea of transmitting using two antenna and receiving with one provides a similar performance as described by the maximal-ratio receiver combing (MRRC)- a type of complex receiver diversity. With his scheme, we can reap the benefits of receiver diversity in a multipath time varying channel at the same cost of complexity. However, there is an

This paper was composed and submitted for review to the ESRA 2013

added advantage of reduced receiver infrastructure. Alamouti proposed that transmit diversity provides the same trend in bit error rate performance with an expenditure of an additional 3dB signal to noise ratio (SNR) than MRRC. In-spite of this added expenditure of 3dB in signal-to-noise ratio requirement, transmit diversity scheme is more lucrative and practical. Alamouti's scheme calls for enhancing the base-stations with more antennae than providing more receive antennae at the remote units, which are large in number. [1]

II. THEORY

A. Equivalence between MRRC and Transmit Diversity

Although Maximal-Ratio Receiver combing and Transmit Diversity bear huge differences in the computation regarding retrieval of a bit and infrastructure i.e. orientation of the multiple antenna, they bear remarkably similar results due to a pivotal concept known as Space-Time Encoding. This can be observed in *Figure II.1*.It shows the Monte Carlo Simulation of a Binary Phase Shift Keying (BPSK) transmission system with no diversity, MRRC and Transmit diversity. In order to observe the manipulation required that makes transmit diversity work, we need to delve in to the requirements of maximal-ratio combining. In Addition, it is necessary that we familiarize ourselves with what space-time coding channel estimation and channel impulse response are

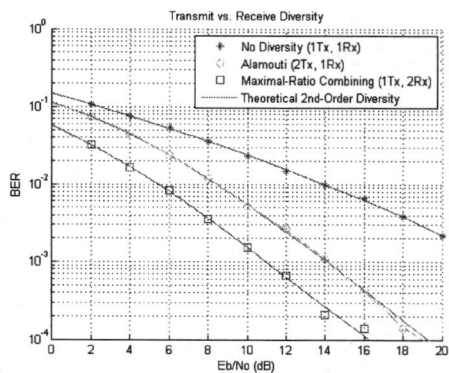

Figure II.1Monte Carlo Simulation of MRRC v/s Transmit Diversity [2]

B. Space Time Coding

Space-time encoding helps spread our data in space and time. This concept of spatial distribution helps us retrieve symbols after combining. The available data is first distributed in space. As a result, we establish multiple channels to transmit on.

Subsequently, we reproduce conjugates of the same data as described in *Figure II.2* and switch them up on the two available channels. [1]. The available symbols S_0 and S_1 are served for encoding at time intervals t and $t+T$ respectively, where T is the time period of each complete symbol. The symbols are then sent separately over two channels during time interval t. In our example, S_0 will be sent over *channel₁* and S_1 over *channel₂*. In the next interval $t+T$, we need to send conjugates of the previous symbols, S_0^* and $-S_1^*$. However, the negative conjugate of S_1 i.e. $-S_1^*$ is sent over *channel₁* and S_0^* is sent over *channel₂*

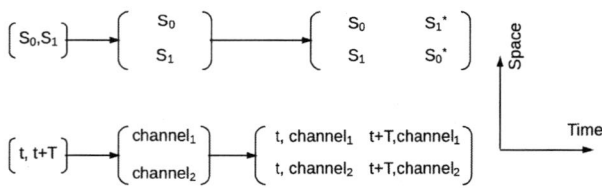

Figure II.2 Space Time Distribution of the symbols

C. Channel Estimation

Channel Sounding is a process that is commonly employed to obtain the channel impulse response. This process is heavily dependent on using Pseudo Random Noise (PN) Sequences. PN sequences are binary sequences that have peculiar properties and are produced using Linear Feedback Shift Registers (LFSR). In brief, to serve the purpose of channel sounding, a PN sequence is transmitted over a channel. This is received and correlated with the same PN sequence. This process is employed because autocorrelation between the same PN sequences gives very evincing results. Since, PN sequences are binary in nature, their autocorrelation behavior can be deducted by studying how an example

1) PN sequence example

For example, lets consider a PN sequence of the degree $N=2$ degrees and polynomial $x^2 + x + 1$. We get a sequence of length $L=2^N - 1=3$. This means that the sequence itself is periodic over $L=3$. The shift register array that provides this code and its initial state is described in *Figure II.5*. The process of generation of a PN sequence is described in Table I.

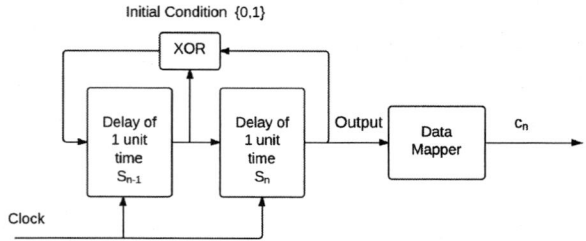

Figure II.3 LFSR to produce a PN sequence of order 2

Hence the transmitted pseudo random sequence is given by a sequence of random pulses described by the following equation (8). Where c_n correspond to the bits associated with the PN sequence, T_c is the chip time of the PN sequences. Chip Time is defined as the time interval of every bit within a PN sequence.

TABLE I
GENERATION OF PN SEQUENCE USING LFSR

Time, n	S_{n-1}, x	S_n, x^2	Output	C_n
-1	0	1	-	-1
0	1	0	1	1
1	1	1	0	-1
2	0	1	1	-1
3	1	0	1	1
4	1	1	0	-1
5	0	1	1	-1
6	1	0	1	-1

$$c(t) = \sum_{n=0}^{\infty} c_n r$$

(8)

Evidently, the sequence $c(t)$ is periodic with period $Tb = 3Tc$. The autocorrelation function of $c(t)$, defined as

$$R_c(\tau) = \frac{1}{T_b} \int_{t_o}^{t_o+T_b} c(t)c(t-\tau)dt \qquad (9)$$

$$R_c(\tau) = \begin{cases} (1 - \dfrac{N+1}{NT_c}), |\tau| < T_c \\ -\dfrac{1}{N}, |\tau| < T_c \end{cases} \qquad (10)$$

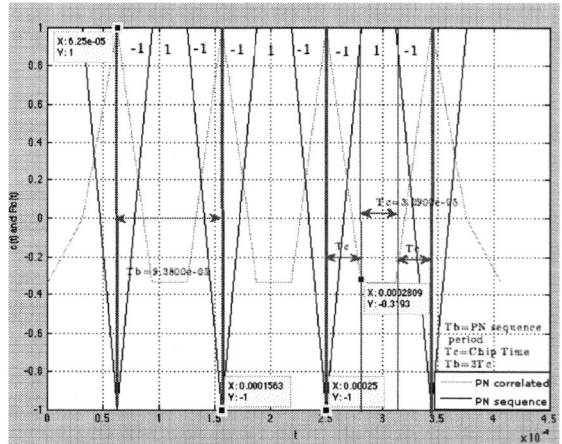

Figure II.6 : PN sequence and its Autocorrelation

Remarkably $R_c(\tau)$ is also periodic with period $T_b = NT_c$, N = 3, and shown below against the PN sequence. The following sequence in described in Table I was recreated using the transmitted symbols from the USRP boards. As can be observed from *Figure II.6*, the PN sequence has a time period T_b, of about 9.38e-5 secs and T_c of about 3.09e-5 secs.

D. Channel Impulse Response

1) Multipath in Wireless Transmission

Consider a channel $h(t)$, to which we subject a PN sequence $c(t)$. The channel $h(t)$ brings about certain changes to $c(t)$. Ideally in a free space system where there exist just one line of sight component between the transmitter and receiver the response of the channel appears as described in *Figure II.7*:

$$c(t), R_c(\tau) \qquad\qquad\qquad c(t), R_c(\tau)$$

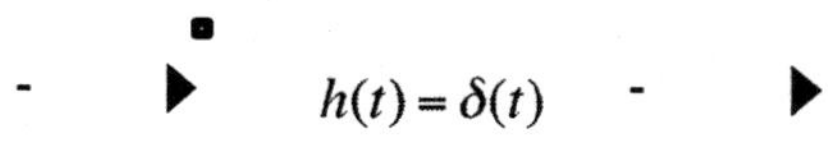

$$h(t) = \delta(t)$$

Figure II.7 Channel model with only Line of sight.

As a result, there is no modification in the PN sequence. The above channel represents a channel in which the transmitted wave doesn't suffer any reflection. Therefore, the autocorrelation at the input will be the same as the autocorrelation at the output. Now consider a channel in which the transmitted wave undergoes reflections. The impulse response is given by $h(t)$ and the channel appears as follows

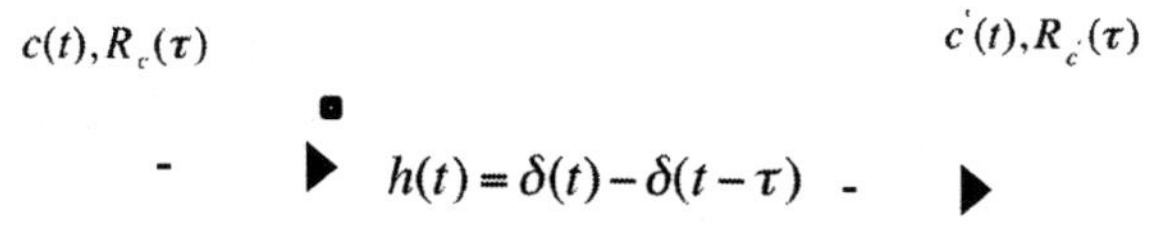

$$c(t), R_c(\tau) \qquad\qquad c'(t), R_{c'}(\tau)$$

$$h(t) = \delta(t) - \delta(t - \tau)$$

Figure II.8 Channel Impulse Response with multiple paths.

Where $c'(t) = c(t) * h(t)$. $\qquad\qquad$ (11)

Convolving $c'(t)$ by $c'(-t)$ we get

$$c'(t) * c'(-t) = (c(t) * h(t)) * (c(-t) * h(-t)) \qquad (12)$$

$$c'(t) * c'(-t) = c(t) * c(-t) * h(t) * h(-t) \qquad (13)$$

$$R_{c'}(\tau) = R_c(\tau) * R_h(\tau) \qquad\qquad (14)$$

Since, $x(t) * x(-t) = R_h(\tau) \qquad\qquad (15)$

Therefore, $R_{c'}(\tau) = R_c(\tau) * h(\tau)$ for observational purposes.

2) Delay Spread
Delay spread equals the time delay between the arrival of the first received signal component (LOS or multipath) and the last received signal component associated with a single transmitted pulse. Another characteristic of the multipath channel is its time-varying nature. This time variation arises because either the transmitter or the receiver is moving, and therefore the location of reflectors in the transmission path, which give rise to multipath, will change over time. [4]

E. Maximal-Ratio Receiver Combining
Maximal-Ratio-Receiver combing is one of the most complex combing techniques. The retrieval of bits is dependent on the successful estimation of the channel. The two channels established between the lone transmitter and the two receivers have the impulse responses h_0 and h_1. On being received by the receiver, the received signal needs to be compensated for the channel effect by multiplying it with the conjugates of the respective impulse responses. The received symbols are:

$$r_0 = h_0 S + n_0 \qquad\qquad (16)$$

$$r_1 = h_1 S + n_1 \qquad\qquad (17)$$

Using the conjugates of the channel estimates we render the effects of the channel neutralized. It only manifests itself in the

form of a scalar magnitude. The receiver combining effect can be summarized as follows.

$$h_0^* r_0 = h_0^*(h_0 S + n_0) = h_0^* h_0 S + h_0^* n_0 = |h_0|^2 S + h_0^* n_0 \qquad (18)$$

$$h_1^* r_1 = h_1^*(h_1 S + n_1) = h_1^* h_1 S + h_1^* n_1 = |h_1|^2 S + h_1^* n_1 \qquad (19)$$

Thus, we obtain the original signal that was originally transmitted. However, it is only scaled by the magnitude of the impulse response. The noise too is affected by the channel estimates [4].

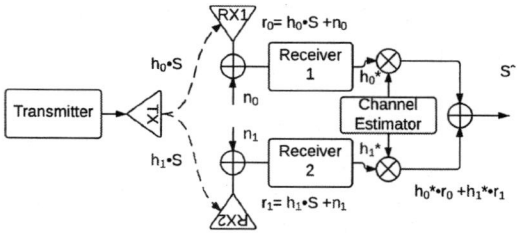

Figure II.4 MRRC Architecture.

F. Transmit Diversity
Transmit Diversity can be described by the arrangement shown in the *Figure II.11* below. We send two independent symbols on two separate antennae. The two successive symbols on the same antennae are not independent of the frames sent before them. They are derived from the first two symbols sent previously. They are conjugates of the previous symbols. This brings us to the fascinating new concept as space-time encoding. The bits sent are S_0 and S_1.

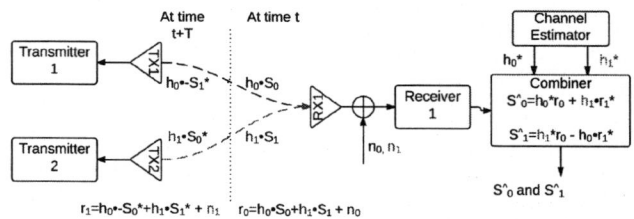

Figure II.10 Transmit Diversity Architecture.

The received signals at time t and $t+T$ the following.

$$r_0 = h_0 S_0 + h_1 S_1 \qquad\qquad (20)$$

$$r1 = -h_0 S_1^* + h_1 S_0^* \qquad\qquad (21)$$

The received symbols are then combined with the channel estimates in the following manner.

$$h_0^* r_0 + h_1 r_1^* \qquad\qquad (22)$$

$$h_1^* r_0 - h_0 r_1^* \qquad\qquad (23)$$

The result of that is as follows.

$$h_0^*(h_0 S_0 + h_1 S_1 + n_0) + h_1(-h_0 S_1^* + h_1 S_0^* + n_1)^* \qquad (24)$$

$$h_1^*(h_0 S_0 + h_1 S_1 + n_0) - h_0(-h_0 S_1^* + h_1 S_0^* + n_1)^* \qquad (25)$$

$$|h_0|^2 S_0 + h_0^* h_1 S_1 + h_0^* n_0 - h_1 h_0^* S_1 + |h_1|^2 S_0 + h_1 n_1^* \qquad (26)$$

$$h_1^* h_0 S_0 + |h_1|^2 S_1 + h_1^* n_0 + |h_0|^2 S_1 - h_0 h_1^* S_0 - h_0 n_1^* \qquad (27)$$

After combining, what remains are the scaled symbols. The scaling is nothing but the combined magnitude of the two complex channels. The accompanying noise is colored by the channel estimates,which is similar to MRRC.

$$(|h_0|^2 + |h_1|^2)S_0 + h_0^* n_0 + h_1 n_1 \qquad (28)$$

$$(|h_0|^2 + |h_1|^2)S_1 + h_0^* n_0 - h_1 n_1^* \qquad (29)$$

III. THE SETUP

The test bed is comprised of two setups, one for transmission and the other for reception. We will consider each of them one by one. *Figure III.1* describes the setup required.

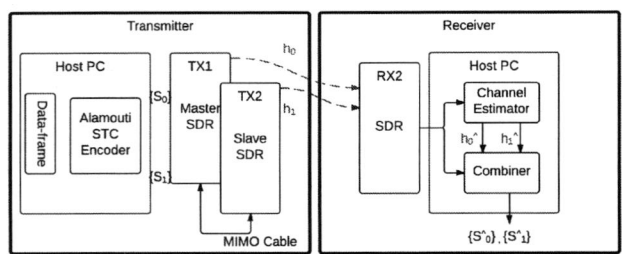

Figure III.1 The Laboratory Setup

A.   Transmitter

The transmitting station consists of the host PC connected to one of the software-defined radios (SDRs) with the help of a gigabit Ethernet cable. The two SDRs are further connected to one another through a Multiple Input Multiple output (MIMO) connection. (Refer *Figure III.1*). The host PC on the transmitter side is responsible for constructing the data frame and space-time encoding. The data-frame is then distributed over two SDRs. The two SDRs are synchronized using the MIMO cable. The two transmitters establish two channels with impulse responses h_0 and h_1 between the transmitting setup and receiving setup.

B.   Receiver

The receiving station consists of a similar setup. However, just one SDR is connected to a host PC using the Ethernet cable. (Refer Figure 3). The host PC on the receiver side is responsible for channel estimation and retrieval of the symbols through combining. The channel estimator constantly spits out the estimated channel responses $\hat{h_0}$ and $\hat{h_1}$ used in combining.

IV.   EQUIPMENT

The equipment used in this experiment are as follows.
- Software Defined Radios – Universal software defined radio peripheral (USRP2) from Ettus Research.
- Host PC – Running Windows XP.
- Simulation Tools – Simulink Mathworks- 2011b.

Software Defined Radios are devices that is capable of operating on a range of frequencies, with variable gains and programmable modulation scheme. They are composed of a mother board and a RF front-end. The specification of one such SDR is given a follows.

A.   USRP2 Specifications

USRP2 devices have the following specifications

- Mother Board
  - 2 ADC 100MS/s (14---bit) [1]
  - 2 DAC 400MS/s (16---bit)
  - Gigabit Ethernet Interface [2]
  - Larger FPGA2
  - On---board SRA
  - MIMO

[1] USRP2 is capable of processing signals up to 100 MHz wide.
[2] USRP2 has Gbps high---speed serial interface for expansion.

- RF Daughterboard
  - RFX-900
    The RFX900 daughter board is capable of supporting a frequency range of 750MHz to 1050MHz.

1)   USRP2 Operational Parameters
The USRP2 has the following three programmable operational parameters.

a)   Frequency
USRP2 is an RF front-end that does the up-conversion and down-conversion of the baseband signal produced on the host PC. The frequency for up-conversion is specified through the host PC and must lie between the specified frequency range of the respective RF daughter board. The daughterboard used for this experiment is RFX900.

b)   Gain
The gain can be specified through the host PC. It is specified in dB and must be limited so as to not saturate the receivers. Saturating the receiver results in the observation of non-linear behavior on the receiving side.

c)   Decimation and Interpolation
The decimation and interpolation factor must be maintained consistent on both sides. The decimation and interpolation dictate the sampling frequency of the SDR. Since, the upper limit of the frequency that can be processed is 100MHz. Hence we need to conserve the frequency of signal being fed to the SDRs. The frequency of the baseband signal is thus dependent on the data rate. Thus, we need to observe the following conservation As a result, the sampling frequency is given by the following equation.

$$\frac{symbol}{s} \times \frac{samples}{symbol} \times I = 100MHz \qquad (25)$$

The sampling time is given by the reciprocal of the sampling frequency.

$$F_s = \frac{samples}{s} = \frac{100MHz}{I} = \frac{1}{T_s} \qquad (26)$$

d)   Frame Length
The USRP is capable of transmitting frames of data. The receiving end provides provision to accept a certain data length depending on the specified frame length. It can be set to any integer value. By default, it is set to 365,which is the length of the payload length of 1500 byte MTU of the Ethernet protocol

V.   TRANSMITTER OPERATION

The transmitter operation carried out on the host PC consist of the following

- Data Frame Construction.
- Alamouti Space Time Encoding.

We choose an Interpolation factor of 512 hence our sample time is given by the following.

$$T_s = \frac{I}{100MHz} = \frac{512}{100MHz} = 0.512e-5s \qquad (27)$$

We however use an actual sampling time of 4000 times the original sample time. As a result, it is 0.0819 seconds. The chip time of the PN sequences used is also the same. It is sufficiently large compared to the coherence time. Therefore, the channels varies slowly as compared to the symbol time. The carrier frequency is decided to by 868MHz and with transmitter gain of 44dB. In Summary, the following device parameters are programmed on the USRP2 on the transmitter side as shown in *Table II*

TABLE II
TRANSMITTER OPERATIONAL PARAMETERS

Parameter	VALUE
Frequency	868MHz
Gain	44dB
Interpolation Factor	512
Sample Time	0.0819 seconds
Chip Time	0.0819 seconds.
Frequency	Value
Gain	868MHz

A. Data Construction

- We transmit a data stream of 1023 bits of sample time appended with 380 header bits.
- The header bits consist of a PN sequence, which is padded with zeros to make an equivalent length of 380 bits.
- The first frame consists of a PN sequence of order 6 and length 63. It is followed with a zero padding of 317 bits to conserve the header length of 380 bits. This header is then affixed in front of a data frame of size 1023 bits,which is the first symbol frame {S1}.
- The second frame consists of a PN sequence of order 7 and length 127. A zero padding of length 253 bits to maintain the header length of 380 bits succeeds it. A data frame of length 1023 is attached to this header as payload. It is the second symbol frame {S2}.
- As portrayed in *Figure V.1*, the two payload frames are PN sequences of order 10 and length 1023 bits. A PN sequence is used to compare the received signal for performance measurements. The payload data frames are modulated using Differential Binary Phase Shift keying (DBPSK).
- Thus, we have a frame of length 2806 bits to be processed by the Alamouti Space Time Encoder.

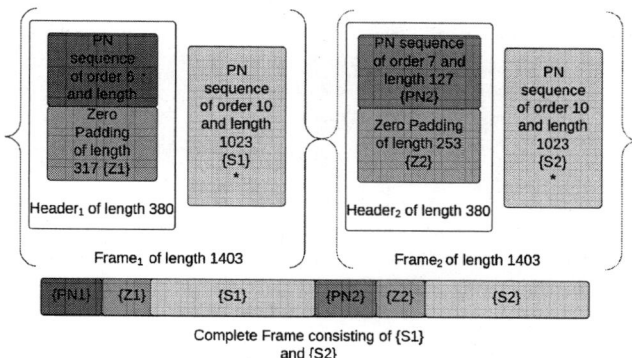

Figure V.1 Data Construction.

B.   Alamouti's Space Time Encoding.

- The complete frame fed to the combiner unit on the transmitter side is bifurcated into its constituent individual frames for the purpose of encoding.
- The next step in the encoding is to strip the individual frames off their headers. This is done so as to maintain integrity of the PN sequence. As it is needed, on the receiver side for channel estimation.
- The payload data frames {S1} and {S2} are now split in space and need to be encoded in time to be distributed over their respective antenna. This is done by producing their conjugates and associating each bit and its successive conjugate bit with the respective antenna.
- Now that the data has been encoded we need to interleave it with the respective headers. Each antenna carries both the PN sequence. As a result, we need to make the same organized complete frame that came in to the combiner.
- Thus ,each antenna carries a frame of length 2806 bits after encoding. The composite time period required to deliver two frames is maintained on the two transmitting antennae.

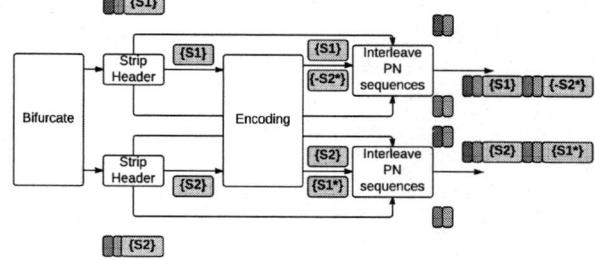

Figure V.2 Alamouti Encoding

VI.   RECEIVER OPERATION

The receiver operations carried out on the host PC at the receiver are as follows.

- Channel Estimation
- Combining

The USRP on the transmitter side is programmed with the following parameters. We use the same sample time on the receiver side. We do use a factor 'd' for oversampling. It can assume any integer value and thus the sample time becomes T_s/d. This will make the receive frame to be d times in length. However, we use d as 1. It is absolutely imperative that the carrier frequency must be similar to that on the receiver side for successful down-conversion. The decimation factor must match the corresponding interpolation factor on the transmitter side. In summary, the USRP2 is programmed using the following device parameters shown in Table III

TABLE III
RECEIVER OPERATIONAL PARAMETERS

Parameter	VALUE
Frequency	868MHz
Gain	44dB
Decimation Factor	512
Sample Time	0.0819 seconds
Frame Length	2806

A. Channel Estimation

The process of channel estimation involves correlating the received signal with the PN sequences used in the header. We then observe the peaks that result out of correlation and extract the complex channel gains. The above process is carried out using the following steps.

- The correlation is performed using matched filters tuned to the PN sequences used in the header frames. The incoming signal is sent to two branches, one have a matched filter tuned to the one with order 6 and the other tuned to the matched filter with the order 7. The matched filters are constructed employing digital filters. The coefficients of the matched filters are selected such that it is a flipped version of the PN sequence.
- After passing the absolute value of the signal through the match filter, we observe peaks on the other side. The peaks coincide with the respective PN sequence placement.
- The matched filter tuned to the PN sequence of order 6 gives peaks due to the PN sequence of order 6.
- The matched filter tuned to the PN sequence of order 7 gives peaks due to the PN sequence of order 7.
- The peaks thus obtained are then normalized and subjected to a threshold value.
- If they pass the threshold, they are then zoomed into through oversampling. We oversample the peaks and find out the value where they are roughly constant and then extract the corresponding complex values.
- These complex channel values are then fed to the Alamouti combiner.

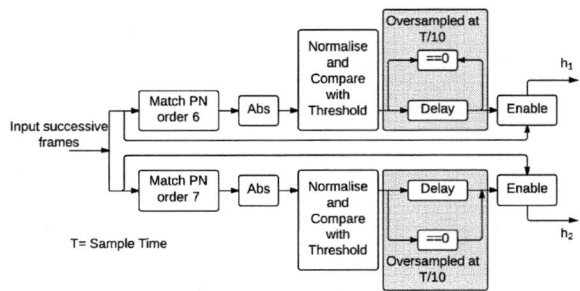

Figure VI.1 Channel Estimation

B. Combining

Once we are furnished with the channel estimates, we need to put the two frames together. While the channel estimator finds the channel parameters on one branch of the receiver operations, we condition the received frames to be further processed by the combiner.

- Similar to the encoding process, the incoming signal is bifurcated into two frames and we strip each frame of its header. Thus, the incoming signal of length 2806 is split into 2 streams of 1403 bit length.
- Subsequently, we unwrap the 380-bit length header and the frames are thus ready for combining.
- The payload frames are combined with the channels estimates in the following fashion.
- After the time period of two frames has elapsed , we are able to construct the two original frames that were sent.

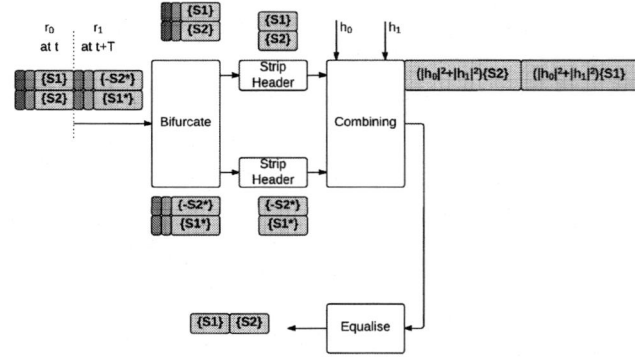

Figure VI.2 Alamouti Combining

VII. PERFORMANCE AND RESULTS

A. PN Correlation.

We were able to successfully estimate the channel using the proposed scheme. Figure VII.1 and FigureVII.2 give the correlated output of the channel estimator.
Figure VII. 1 bears just the alternate bursts of PN sequences.
In this case, we only send the two PN sequences, the rest of the data is zero. The top window shows the matched filter output of the correlator that is tuned to the PN sequence of length 63 .The second window is the received signal. The third window is the filter output of the matched filter of the correlator that is tuned to

the PN sequence for length 127.As can be observed, we see correlation at alternate bursts. It can be easily interpreted that PN sequence of length 63 is followed by a PN sequence of length 127 and this combination is repeated.

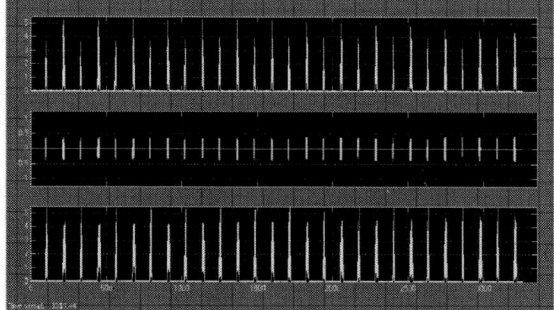

Figure VII.1 Autocorrelation of just PN sequences

Figure VII.2 is the result when we send the headers followed by payload data of length 1023 bits. We can see the bursts received and separate the zero padding. The first window is the output of the matched filter tuned to the PN sequence of order 6 –length 63 and the second window is just the burst being received. The third window is the output of the matched filter tuned to the PN sequence of order 7- length 127.

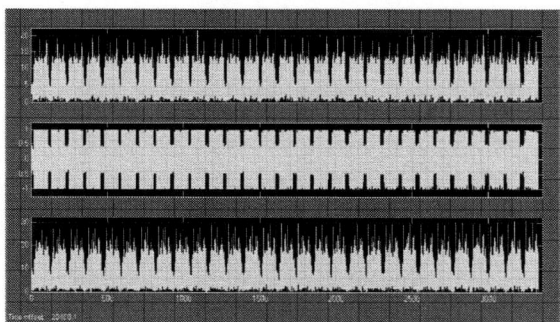

Figure VII.2 Autocorrelation of complete frame

B. Demodulation.

The channel coefficients thus obtained are used to combine the frames together and given to the DBPSK modulator. The output of the DBPSK modulator is explained in *Figure VII.3*. As can be evidently seen, we are able to gain a sense of DBPSK from *Figure VII.3*.

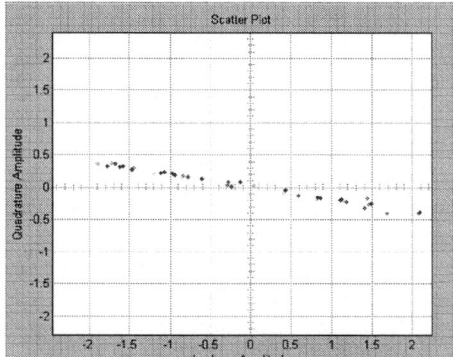

Figure VII.4 Demodulation of the payload

VIII. FUTURE WORK

A. Frame Synchronisation

Presently the receiver has no sense of timing. We need to incorporate that to achieve the complete results. Since there are 3 remote units involved, each of them have their respective local oscillators. This manifests itself in the relative drift between the clocks and hence it may so happen that we process a frame midway as opposed to the beginning.

We need to device a technique for choosing data bits after the correlation peaks and open a widow for streaming for a length of (1023 + the padded zeroes). This will ensure that we combine the encoded symbols without any offset in the received streamed data

IX. REFERENCES

[1]   Siavash M. Alamouti. "A Simple Transmit Diversity Technique for Wireless Communications",IEEE JOURNAL ON SELECT AREAS IN COMMUNICATIONS, VOL. 16, NO. 8, OCTOBER 1998.

[2]   *Introduction to MIMO systems*, Mathworks Matlab. Natick, Massachusetts, U.S.A. 1984.

[3]   Simon Haykin, "Communication Systems", 4th Edition Wiley

[4]   Andrea Goldsmith, "Wireless Communications" 2005 Cambridge University Press

Anaam Ansari is a graduate student at Charles W. Davidson College of Engineering, San Jose State University in the Electrical Engineering Department. She obtained her undergraduate degree, Bachelor of Engineering – Electronics (B.E) from the University of Mumbai in the year 2011.
Email Address: anaam.ansari@sjsu.edu

Dr. Robert Morelos Zaragoza is professor at the Charles W. Davidson College of Engineering, San Jose State University inthe Electrical Engineering Department. He has research interests in the areas of error correcting codes and digital signal processing techniques for wireless communication systems. He is the author of twenty international peer-reviewed journal papers, more than eighty international conference papers and the book *The Art of Error Correcting Coding* (2nd edition, John Wiley and Sons, 2006). Prof. Morelos-Zaragoza holds eighteen patents in the U.S.A., Japan and Europe, on the topics of error correcting coding (ECC) and cognitive radio (CR). Robert is a senior member of the IEEE, an active consultant for industry in ECC and CR technologies, and serves as reviewer, editor and technical program committee member in numerous international IEEE conferences and journals in Information Theory and Wireless Communication Systems.
Email Adress: robert.morelos-zaragoza@sjsu.edu.

SESSION

DEVELOPING RECONFIGURABLE HETEROGENEOUS SYSTEMS

Chair(s)

TBA

Int'l Conf. Reconfigurable Systems and Algorithms | ERSA'13 |

29

Heuristically Driven Task Agglomeration in Limited Resource Partially-Reconfigurable Systems

David Austin[1], B. Earl Wells[1],

[1]Dept. of Electrical and Computer Engineering, Univ. of Alabama in Huntsville, Huntsville, Alabama, USA

Abstract—*This paper introduces a method for enhancing run time performance of a dynamic partially reconfigurable system. The technique is applied to fully deterministic task systems that are large in comparison to the resources of the target reconfigurable device. Performance improvements are realized by increasing the granularity of the task system at compile time in a manner that reduces the number of context switches that are required during run-time, thereby decreasing the system execution time. Two algorithms are proposed to implement this technique. Both methods are implemented using simulation, and their performance is compared to a sophisticated heuristic scheduler, which reveals a significant improvement in performance.*

Keywords: reconfigurable systems, scheduling, heuristic algorithms

1. Introduction

Partially dynamically reconfigurable systems make use of reconfigurable hardware, such as Field-Programmable Gate Arrays (FPGAs), that are capable of being modified while executing. These systems are attractive since they combine the flexibility of software with the performance of hardware. With careful orchestration, modern systems are reconfigurable at run-time allowing an application to be mapped into a reconfigurable system that is physically smaller than what would normally be necessary to implement the application. A large application can fit into a physically smaller device because parts of the application that are not active can be removed from the device so that other parts of the application can make use of the resources of the device, allowing a type of spatial multiplexing within the device.

The lifecycle of a reconfigurable system can be subdivided into two phases: compile time, and run-time. During compile time, bitstreams are generated, initial configurations are defined and loaded, and static scheduling is performed. In run-time, the generated tasks are executed and reconfigured. The time necessary to generate a new bitstream for a reconfigurable partition can be on the order of minutes. This requires that the synthesis operation be performed at compile time with the system being compiled into separate modular bitstreams for each task.

In order to map the application onto a physically smaller device, it must be divided into discrete functional units, or tasks. However, the fragmentation of the overall application creates a sub-optimal condition since the area allocated to the functional block must be large enough to implement the largest possible function it will ever contain. If the application is partitioned such that there is one large task and many smaller tasks, the spacial efficiency is poor since the extra area available in the hardware goes unused by the majority of the tasks.

Another drawback of this approach is that because of the way reprogramming bitstreams are generated, each bitstream is specifically tied to a given location within the device [1]. To be able to implement all tasks in every reconfigurable region, each region must have an available task implementation that is specifically mapped to that location in the device. This can cause a large number of bitstreams to be generated for the entire application. There has been some work [2] to allow bitstreams to be placed at generic locations in a FPGA, but even then tasks cannot be arbitrarily placed in any functional block. This further restricts the ability to dynamically reprogram the device. Reducing the number of tasks, the number of relocatable regions, or both will reduce the number of combinations required to be generated.

In order to overcome these challenges, this paper presents a method to combine the functional blocks to make more efficient use of the space occupied within a reconfigurable device. This technique is suitable to be run at compile time in order to help improve the performance of the task system. Further, by combining tasks we reduce the number of tasks, which helps to reduce the number of partial bitstreams that are required to implement it in reconfigurable hardware.

2. Background

Scheduling of reconfigurable systems is a very active area of research, and has been mentioned many times [3], [4], [5]. Task clustering has been previously suggested as a means to improve performance of various scheduling techniques. Clustering of software tasks on multiprocessor systems has been considered for some years [6], [7]. Clustering for reconfigurable systems has only been proposed in a few recent papers. In [8], the authors describe a methodology to map an application onto a Network-on-Chip (NoC) to improve communication performance. This is accomplished by combining high communication cost tasks into small

System-on-Chip (SoC) like clusters that then connect to a larger NoC. This technique is primarily concerned with optimizing the inter-task communication by minimizing the communication distance between regularly communicating tasks. The authors of [9] develop a very capable algorithm for clustering tasks as part of a codesign process. However, their approach relies on being able to effectively profile the system's operation. While they do apply this approach to a heterogeneous reconfigurable architecture, they do not apply it to any dynamically reconfigurable systems.

A dynamically reconfigurable clustering technique is proposed in [10]. This approach is similar to the technique that we present in this paper. However, the authors assume that the reconfigurable architecture is large enough to contain the entire application. In their approach, they use a tiered NoC Approach. Tasks are grouped into clusters interconnected with a network switch, and then assigned to a reconfigurable slot, which is connected to the other slots via interslot network switches. This system allows dynamic bitstream generation, and is primarily concerned with improving area utilization, and adding capabilities at run time.

None of the previous research we examined considers the limited resource case where the reconfigurable system needs to be shared to implement the entire application. Consistent with this approach, the primary method considered for improving the runtime is centered on improving the intertask communication performance. The contributions of this paper are a heuristic based task combination algorithm that is suitable for improving the runtime of a reconfigurable system in a limited resource, nonpreemptive, partially reconfigurable hardware environment.

2.1 Definitions

A task is a discrete set of operations executed in order that transforms an input into an output. Tasks generally have data dependencies as well as control dependencies. If a task is data dependent on another task, the dependent task is said to be a data dependency sink task, whereas the other task is said to be a data dependency source task.

Tasks are described by several metrics which include: the task area, which is the amount of reconfigurable resources needed to implement the task; the execution time of the task; and the time required to reconfigure (context switch) the device for the task. It is assumed that the context switching time is comparatively long relative to the execution time, which imposes a significant penalty on context switching. Given this long switching time we do not consider the preemptive case where a task is interrupted before it completes execution.

Each task also has a type; the task's type represents the specific set of actions the task performs. Tasks with the same type perform the same operations, however, the data that the task operates on is expected to differ between instantiations. As an example, in a signal processing application a type may represent an operation such as a Fourier Transform that is run multiple times during the course of the application.

An application is an arrangement of tasks such that the data and control dependencies are met in a meaningful way to accomplish a specific purpose. Therefore, an application can be modeled as a directed acyclic graph. The graph (application) G can be visualized as a tuple, $G = (T, E_d)$, where T is the set of tasks, E_d is the set of directed edges that represent data flow, [11].

A dynamically configurable platform represents the complete hardware execution environment for the application. The platform consists of multiple Processing Elements (PEs) used to execute individual tasks. In general, there will be both software PEs (traditional microprocessors) and hardware PEs (FPGAs) in a reconfigurable system. Only hardware PEs are considered in this paper.

Since the PEs are partially dynamically reconfigurable, each PE is comprised of one or more partially reconfigurable partitions, which are the minimum reconfigurable unit of the PE. Generally, these partitions are heterogeneous in size, however, for the purposes of this paper it is assumed that the partitions are homogeneous in size.

Each PE partition has a limited number of reconfigurable resources available to implement tasks. These are classified into two principal categories: routing resources and processing resources. Both types of resources are consumed by implementing a task; it is assumed that the processing resources are the dominating constraint.

2.2 Practical Partially Reconfigurable Architectures

Current FPGAs support a limited partial reconfiguration; the partitions can contain an arbitrary number of columns, but have fixed row division boundaries. Fig. 1 shows an example PE that has a single fixed row division. In this example, a partition can be any number of columns wide, but must either be less than half the height of the device, or occupy the entire height of the device. Of course, it follows that the size of the largest task dictates the minimum size of a PE partition.

For partial dynamic reconfiguration to work, the device must be divided into static and dynamically reconfigurable regions. The static areas are used to implement such functions as reconfiguration control logic and I/O, both between the various reconfigurable regions and outside the PE. In Fig.1, the static regions are shown as the dark shaded areas, while the lighter areas represent the dynamically reconfigurable areas.

Another practical restriction on the capabilities of existing hardware is the number of simultaneous reconfigurations a device may support. Typical hardware limits the number of such reconfigurations because there are a limited number of reconfiguration controllers. In this paper, we do not restrict the number of simultaneous reconfigurations.

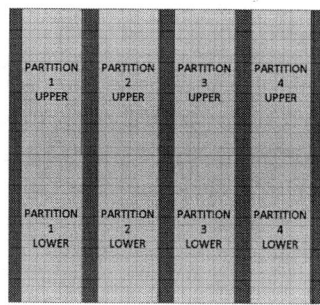

Figure 1: Example Processing Element

3. Theory of Operation

It is envisioned that the technique described in this paper is capable of producing schedules that are significantly better (smaller makespan) than schedules of unmodified task systems. Further, the approach should not decrease the performance of any task system during run-time. This technique does impose a level of computational overhead, but it is only incurred once for each task system, at compile time, which is not generally time critical.

To justify the computational overhead of the clustering algorithm, graphs should be selected to maximize the effectiveness of clustering. Clustering should be most effective on graphs that experience a significant amount of reconfiguration. Likely the optimum value is a function of the number of PEs, and the average size of tasks relative to the area available in a PE partition.

3.1 Formalization of Rules

We make the following observations and assumptions relative to applications, tasks, and PEs:

1) The number of PEs and partitions is set before run-time.
2) The application is large relative to the size of the partition, such that the entire application cannot be realized in the available reconfigurable resources at one time.
3) The time to reconfigure a partition is a function of the size of the partition.
4) Task types represent a specific sequence of operations. Tasks with the same type id differ only in the data processed.
5) Subsequent executions of tasks with the same type id within the same PE do not require reconfiguration.
6) Each PE partition can have exactly one active task at any given time.
7) Even though only one task is active at a time more than one task can be present within a partition. If so, we declare this to be a task cluster.
8) At compile time, tasks can be divided into groups such that the resultant grouping will fit into at least 1 PE partition.
9) Subsequent execution of different tasks within the same cluster doesn't require a reconfiguration.
10) Resources within a cluster are only consumed once per instance.

Given the above, we conclude that it should be possible to combine 2 or more individual tasks from the task graph into a complex clustered task that performs the functions of the individual constituent tasks. Further, we infer that doing so should improve the run-time of the system because the number of system reconfigurations has been reduced. We also note that the act of clustering tasks is logically equivalent to introducing a new task type. The clustered task's type serves to identify which of the constituent tasks are included in the cluster.

It should be noted that when tasks are clustered they do not lose their identities. Only the type is altered to match the other tasks in the same cluster. When a PE must be reconfigured to bring in a new task, the tasks that are likely to be needed next are many times brought into that same partition instead of padding the configuration bitstream.

4. Example Task System

We now consider an illustrative example to demonstrate the proposed concept. Consider the application and reconfigurable platform shown in Fig. 2. The task system consists of 3 tasks executing on a single PE with 2 reconfigurable regions. Each task is a different type, which is represented by the varying size of each task in the figure. Assume that Task 1 and Task 2 are independent of each other, and that Task 3 is data dependent on the output of Task 2.

Fig. 2a represents an initial task allocation to the available hardware. Since Task 1 and Task 2 are independent, they may begin execution once the hardware is configured and ready. Fig. 2b shows how this application would execute. Both PE partitions begin by reconfiguring for their first task. Once reconfigured, the tasks begin execution. Since Task 1 completes before Task 2, partition 1 can begin reconfiguring to execute Task 3. Task 3 can begin execution as soon as both the reconfiguration is complete and Task 2 completes execution. Since Task 2 completes before the reconfiguration is done for Task 3, Task 3 may begin execution as soon as reconfiguration is complete.

We note from the example that although Task 1 occupies only a small portion of reconfigurable region 1, the entire region is consumed by this task, as shown in Fig. 2a. This mapping represents poor spatial efficiency because reconfigurable region 1 has so much unused space. Alternatively there is the approach presented in Fig. 3. In this scenario, Task 1 and Task 3 have been combined into a single task cluster, which now represents a new fourth task type. Fig. 3b depicts the effect of clustering on the execution of this example task system. As before, Task 1 and Task 2 may begin execution immediately following the completion of the

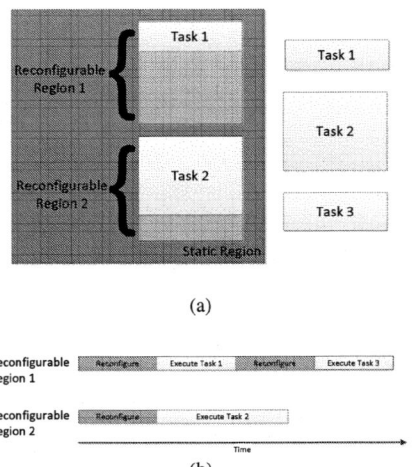

(a)

(b)

Figure 2: Example Task System Before Clustering (a) Physical Implementation and (b) Execution Profile

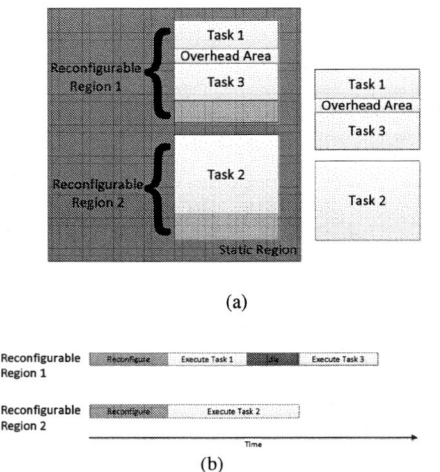

(a)

(b)

Figure 3: Example Task System After Clustering (a) Physical Implementation and (b) Execution Profile

initial reconfiguration, but because Tasks 1 and 3 have been combined into a new task there is no need to reconfigure partition 1 after Task 1 completes execution. However, since Task 3 is dependent on the completion of Task 2, it may not begin to execute until Task 2 has completed. Therefore, an idle period has been introduced before the start of Task 3 to delay its execution until Task 2 has completed.

We see from this example that although the idle time has been introduced, it is for a shorter period than the reconfiguration delay that would have normally occurred. Further, this idle period can be of varying length while the reconfiguration time must always be of the same duration, since a fixed size partition is always being reconfigured.

5. Algorithm Development

The selection of optimal clusters is a topic of consideration. In this paper we present two algorithms that we have developed to generate candidate task clusters. The first uses a simulated annealing heuristic to develop and weigh clusters, while the second uses a straightforward list based methodology to develop a proposed task clustering.

Both clustering algorithms makes use of a sophisticated heuristic based static scheduler to determine an initial schedule. This scheduler has been used in previous research to create good base-line schedules to compare in terms of quality to those produced by less knowledgeable dynamic methodologies [11]. This scheduler utilizes multi-iteration lifecycle heuristics of Particle Swarm, Simulated Annealing, and genetic algorithms to produce its results. In this work we utilize the genetic algorithm methodology exclusively because its parameters were set in a manner that produced significantly better results than the other two methods. The genetic algorithm utilizes a classical multigenerational GA that merges PE assignment and the partial task ordering into a single chromosome. The standard genetic operators of crossover and mutation are performed along with a tournament style selection algorithm. The parameters used in [11] of population size, crossover probability, and mutation probability were identical to those used in this work.

It should be noted that the scheduler has two separate components. One component produces the task ordering which specifies the PE region within the reconfigurable logic that task would execute and the relative order that the task would execute. It does not specify the actual timing though. The second component produces the detailed schedule which includes the task execution time, the idle time, and the task reconfiguration time. It does this in a manner that adheres to the ordering information produced by the ordering component. The fitness function was designed in a manner that minimizes the makespan time. It should be noted that having the two component architecture allows the static scheduler to produce suggested clusters in at least two ways. One by changing the typing information for the given task graph before the scheduling method was invoked and the second method was to modify the task ordering routine to allow tasks to be combined together into new types before the schedule was created.

These are the two approaches described in this paper. Both approaches are based upon the combination of tasks into the same task type only if they fit within the same cluster. To do this, the clustering routine first adjusts the type of both tasks to a new value that differs from any other assigned task type. Then, all graph tasks are searched to find any tasks that correspond to either of the base types of the clustered tasks. These are then updated to also correspond to the newly assigned cluster type. For example, if base types a and b are selected for clustering, all other instances of base type a and b are also converted to the new type. This ensures that if a task with a different task ID but same base type occurs either immediately before or after task a or b, the PE will not have to undergo a reconfiguration if transitioning from the clustered task to one of its constituent tasks or vice versa.

5.1 Simulated Annealing Technique

The first combination algorithm uses a Simulated Annealing heuristic to control the task clustering process. Fig. 4 depicts the flow of this combination algorithm. The algorithm begins with a list of all of the tasks sorted numerically according to their task ID. Then the algorithm selects, at random, a task ID from the list. Starting with the next task ID, each subsequent task is evaluated to determine if the linear combination of the two tasks area will exceed the available resources in the PE partition. If the tasks will fit into the partition, the clustering logic described above is executed.

The algorithm then evaluates the next task ID in the list to see if it can also be added to the cluster. If so, the task is added using the same clustering logic, and advances to the next task. It proceeds in this manner until it reaches the numerically last task ID on the list.

Once the clustering phase is complete, the updated task system is passed back to the static scheduler for evaluation. The result of the static scheduler is compared to the schedule length of the previous task system. If the new system's schedule length is shorter than the previous, it is accepted, and the algorithm proceeds to the next iteration by randomly selecting a new start task ID. In the case that the new schedule is not improved, the new system may be accepted probabilistically. The probability of accepting a worse schedule decreases exponentially with each iteration of the Simulated Annealing algorithm. The schedule component is then rerun assuming this new typing. It will produce a new value that will represent the fitness which will feed back into the Simulated Annealing Algorithm.

5.2 Fixed Order Technique

The second clustering technique uses a simple greedy list based clustering algorithm, as shown in Fig. 5. This clustering algorithm makes use of the static scheduler's ordering and PE allocation phase. Once the static scheduler has determined a task to PE mapping, the clustering algorithm starts with the first task allocated to the first PE. This algorithm examines the area occupied in the PE partition by the task. It then examines the next task to see if both tasks will fit into the partition. If so, the two tasks are combined using the same type conversion logic as the SA approach. The algorithm then proceeds through the remaining tasks assigned to the PE, adding as many tasks to the cluster as possible. The clustering algorithm then proceeds to the tasks assigned to the next PE and tests these tasks for clustering in the same fashion, and so on for the remaining PEs.

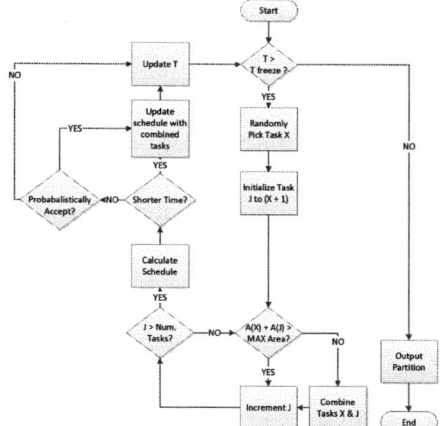

Figure 4: Simulated Annealing Process Flow

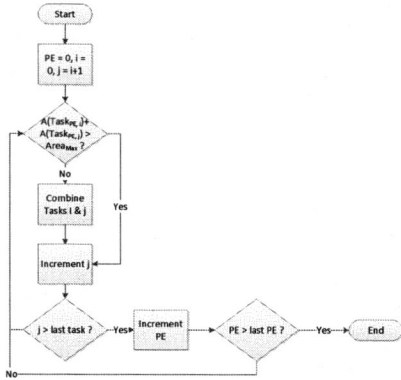

Figure 5: Fixed Order Process Flow

5.3 Analysis

The execution time of a given task graph can be determined by using (1), where n is the number of tasks allocated to a given PE, T_{Ei} is the Execution time of the ith task of the PE, n_R is the number of reconfigurations undergone on that PE, T_R is the fixed reconfiguration time, T_I is the total idle time for the given PE, and the maximum is taken over the PE partitions.

$$max_{PE}\left(\left(\sum_{i=0}^{n}T_{Ei}\right) + n_RT_R + T_I\right) \quad (1)$$

We see from this that there are three components to the run-time of the application. The individual task execution times are spent doing useful computational work, while the rest of the time is in either idle or reconfiguration states. If we impose the restriction that the tasks must have the

Table 1: Simulation Cases

Simulation Case	Partition Size	Algorithm
1	Small	Simulated Annealing
2	Medium	Simulated Annealing
3	Large	Simulated Annealing
4	Small	Fixed Order
5	Medium	Fixed Order
6	Large	Fixed Order

same PE allocation and ordering before and after clustering, a speedup will be realized if the increased idle time does not exceed the decreased reconfiguration time.

6. Results

In order to compare the effects of the clustering algorithms, a set of computer simulations were run to determine the effect of the proposed approach. Performance is established by providing the simulation a number of task graphs representing various applications. The average results are compared against the best available nonclustered schedule, which is provided by the static scheduler before the clustering algorithms are applied.

Task graphs are synthetically generated using Task Graph for Free [12]. To maintain compatibility with earlier work [11], the input task sets are identical to those used previously. A total of 6 simulation cases were run, as shown in Table 1. Each simulation case consists of 40 task graphs with various task and dependency characteristics. The partition size was considered at 3 levels for each clustering algorithm under consideration. The levels were chosen such that the average task size represents 5%, 15%, and 30% of the total partition size. These correspond to the large, medium and small partition cases respectively.

Task characteristics were also synthetically generated using TGFF. Areas are uniformly distributed on $[1,000,5,000)$, while execution times are uniformly distributed on $[2,000,4,000)$. The simulated reconfigurable platform has the following characteristics:

- A single PE with 3 reconfigurable partitions
- Homogeneous partition sizes
- A fixed reconfiguration time, resulting from the homogeneous partition size
- Each reconfigurable partition supports independent simultaneous reconfiguration

7. Discussion and Conclusion

It can be seen from Fig. 6 that this approach does in fact improve the overall task system execution time as measured by the speedup, where the speedup is taken to be the ratio of the clustered graph's execution time to the best known non-clustered execution time (the heuristic static scheduler).

Since the execution times of the individual tasks have not been altered by this approach, the speedup can be

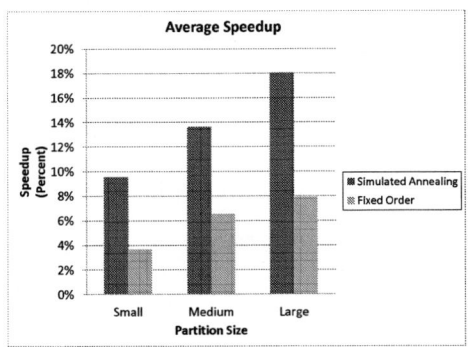

Figure 6: Avg. Speedup of the Clustering Algorithms

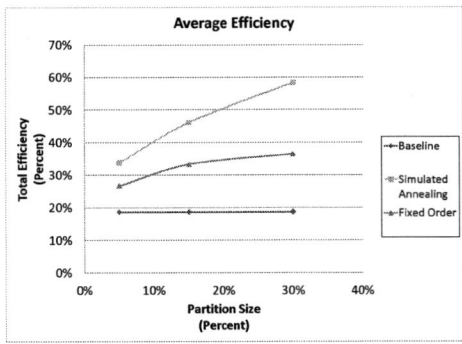

Figure 7: Avg. Efficiency of the Clustering Algorithms

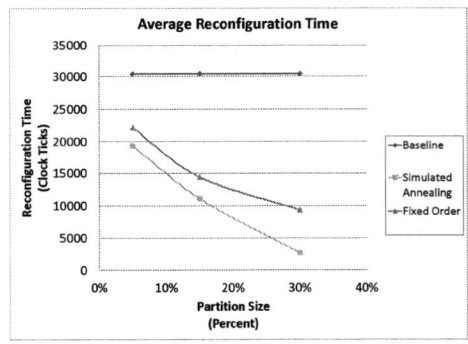

Figure 8: Avg. Reconfiguration Time after Clustering

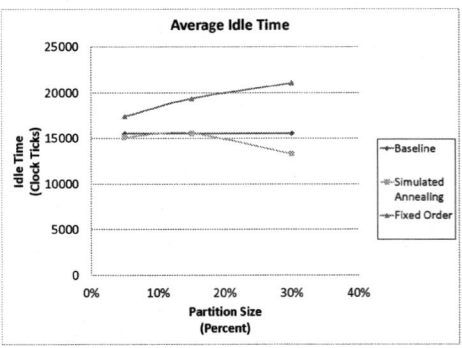

Figure 9: Avg. Idle Time after Clustering

Int'l Conf. Reconfigurable Systems and Algorithms | ERSA'13 |

35

attributed to improved execution efficiency, i.e. less time is spent in non-productive states, which can be seen in Fig. 7. The efficiency is calculated as the ratio of task execution time to total run time. From (1) we see that there are two components that contribute to the nonproductive time, reconfiguration time and idle time. By further analyzing the two unproductive states as shown in Fig. 8 and Fig. 9, we see, as expected, a decrease in the amount of time reconfiguring the device, but an increase in the amount of time that the device is idle due to waiting on precedence constraints that have not been met.

An intuitive result is that decreasing the number of task types below the number of PE partitions does not improve performance significantly. When the number of partitions is equal to the number of task types there is a one to one correspondence between types and partitions. Each partition can implement one task type, and there will be no need to reconfigure them. Although there may still be room in the partition to implement additional tasks, there is no benefit to doing so, since no further reconfigurations will be prevented.

From comparing results between the two proposed algorithms, it can be seen that the heuristic based algorithm outperforms on average the simple fixed order approach. The Simulated Annealing technique benefits from the fact that that every time a proposed task clustering is generated, the static heuristic scheduler is run again. This is necessary to determine the value of the objective function so the simulated annealing heuristic can determine if the clustering has improved the schedule length. However, it also allows the task ordering to be modified, potentially determining an order with less idle time.

We conclude that applying the clustering approach to the limited resource problem is an effective means to improve run-time. Both algorithms presented showed an appreciable speedup. Although the fixed order approach is outperformed by the heuristic approach, the fixed order algorithm benefits from simplicity, resulting in a quicker run-time, especially on large task graphs. Further, in no case did either of the clustering algorithms produce a clustered schedule that exceeded the initial schedule generated by the static scheduler. Therefore, we have met our goal of producing a scheduler that only incurs a compile time penalty and doesn't degrade the run-time performance

8. Further Work

Although the results reported in this paper are encouraging, they represent an initial data set that validates an intuitive concept. These results can be extended in a number of ways. Principally, we would like to evaluate the effectiveness using task graph models extracted from real world applications.

It is expected that some amount of additional resources are used by the resulting clustered task as opposed to the two base tasks. Generally, this overhead would arise from the inference of additional registers to be able to pass data in and out of the individual tasks. Likely this overhead is a small, fixed amount of the combined task resources. Some investigation should be done to determine suitable parameters to characterize this overhead.

Overhead was not considered as part of the simulation, since no task cluster was found to occupy the entirety of a partition following a combination event. Rather than complicate the task combination logic, the overhead can be accounted for by reducing the size of the partition when the tasks are selected for clustering. A further result of tracking overhead in this way would result in tracking different partition sizes for different task clusters, which would be an important advance to considering a reconfigurable platform with heterogeneous PE partitions.

The general task system also includes nondeterministic control dependent tasks along with the deterministic dependencies considered here. For computational simplicity, these control tasks were not considered by this paper. An important improvement to this technique would be to test the effectiveness of the clustering approach against a task system with control dependencies as well as data dependencies.

References

[1] Xilinx, "Partial reconfiguration user guide v14.3," October 2012.

[2] T. Becker, W. Luk, and P. Y. Cheung, "Enhancing relocatability of partial bitstreams for run-time reconfiguration," in *Proc. 2007 IEEE Symp. Field-Programmable Custom Computing Machines*, April 2007, pp. 35 – 44.

[3] J. Resano and D. Mozos, "Specific scheduling support to minimize the reconfiguration overhead of dynamically reconfigurable hardware," in *Proc. 41st annual Design Automation Conference*, 2004, pp. 119–124.

[4] K. Danne and M. Platzner, "An edf schedulability test for periodic tasks on reconfigurable hardware devices," in *ACM SIGPLAN Notices*, vol. 41, no. 7, 2006, pp. 93–102.

[5] S. M. Loo and B. E. Wells, "Applying stochastic static task scheduling to a reconfigurable hardware environment," *Int. Journal Computers and their Applications*, vol. 12, no. 2, pp. 57–75, 2005.

[6] A. Gerasoulis and T. Yang, "On the granularity and clustering of directed acyclic task graphs," *IEEE Trans. Parallel Distrib. Syst.*, vol. 4, no. 6, pp. 686–701, 1993.

[7] M. Palis, J. Liou, and D. Wei, "A greedy task clustering heuristic that is provably good," in *1994 Int. Symp. Parallel Architectures, Algorithms and Networks, (ISPAN)*, 1994, pp. 398–405.

[8] F. Fangfa, B. Yuxin, H. Xinaan, W. jinxiang, Y. Minyan, and Z. Jia, "An objective-flexible clustering algorithm for task mapping and scheduling on cluster-based noc," in *2010 Academic Symp. Optoelectronics and Microelectronics Technology and 10th Chinese-Russian Symp. Laser Physics and Laser Technology*, 2010, pp. 369–373.

[9] S. Ostadzadeh, R. Meeuws, K. Sigdel, and K. Bertels, "A multipurpose clustering algorithm for task partitioning in multicore reconfigurable systems," in *2009 Int. Con. on Complex, Intelligent and Software Intensive Systems. (CISIS '09).*, March 2009, pp. 663 –668.

[10] I. Beretta, V. Rana, D. Atienza, and D. Sciuto, "Run-time mapping of applications on fpga-based reconfigurable systems," in *Proc. 2010 IEEE International Symp. Circuits and Systems (ISCAS)*, May 30-June 2 2010, pp. 3329 –3332.

[11] Z. Pan and B. Wells, "Hardware supported task scheduling on dynamically reconfigurable SOC architectures," *IEEE Trans. VLSI Syst.*, vol. 16, no. 11, pp. 1465 –1474, Nov. 2008.

[12] R. P. Dick, D. L. Rhodes, and W. Wolf, "TGFF: Task graphs for free," in *Proc. 6th Int. Workshop Hardware/Software Codesign (CODES/CASHE '98)*, 1998, pp. 97–101.

An Automatic Design and Implementation Framework for Reconfigurable Logic IP Core

Qian Zhao, Motoki Amagasaki, Masahiro Iida, Morihiro Kuga and Toshinori Sueyoshi
Graduate School of Science and Technology, Kumamoto University

Abstract— *Conventional full-custom reconfigurable logic device design and implementation are time consuming processes. In this research, we propose a design framework in order to improve FPGA IP core design efficiency by link academic FPGA design flow and commercial VLSI CADs based on the synthesizable method. A novel FPGA routing tool is developed in this framework, namely the EasyRouter. By using simple templates, EasyRouter can automatically generate the HDL codes and the configuration bitstream for an FPGA. With this design flow, accurate physical information can be reported when a new FPGA architecture is evaluated with reliable commercial VLSI CADs. For FPGA architectures that cannot be easily implemented with present VLSI process, EasyRouter provides a fast performance analysis flow, which improved delay accuracy 5.1 times than VPR on average.*

1. Introduction

Embedded systems play an increasingly important part in electronic products. In particular, system-on-a-chip (SoC) technology has developed rapidly. A variety of functions can be implemented by embedding various hard intellectual property (IP) cores in a single silicon die. However, a new product must be fabricated with an entirely new mask. Even if only small changes are made to a product to improve functionality, a huge cost is incurred. The embedded field-programmable gate array (FPGA) IPs can be used to solve this problem because of their programmability after manufacture.

There are two FPGA IP implement methods. The full-custom FPGA IP is designed in time-consuming manually process. On the other hand, the synthesizable FPGA IP is designed with automatic application specified integrated circuit (ASIC) flow. In traditional designs, the synthesizable method had much worse area, delay and power performances than the full-custom. However, the performance gaps had been improved significantly in researches such as [1]. Therefore, synthesizable design method is suitable for design efficiency sensitive customizable FPGA IP implementation.

Xilinx and Altera have released their programmable SoC products [2] [3]. A powerful ARM-based processor and universal FPGA fabrics are integrated into one chip to reduce power, cost, and board size. However, the FPGA IP cores from these companies are not customizable and not provided

to other SoC designers. Menta is providing domain-specific synthesizable and hard macro eFPGA core IPs [4]. However, Menta's CAD tools are only designed for their commercial eFPGA IPs. Therefore, CAD tools and a design flow for FPGA IP research and design are necessary.

The contribution of this paper is to propose an FPGA design framework that specifically improves the design efficiency of FPGA IP for SoC. We have developed a simple and automatic FPGA IP design framework that combines FPGA design tools with commercial very-large-scale integration (VLSI) CADs. The FPGA IP that produced by the proposed framework can be directly adopted in SoC design flow as an IP core.

The remainder of this paper is organized as follows. Section 2 introduces related FPGA design flows and issues of traditional design flows. The novel router tool EasyRouter is introduced in Section 3. Section 4 describes the proposed FPGA IP design flow. In Section 5, we first introduce evaluation conditions. Then we compare the performance of EasyRouter with the conventional VPR and then discuss evaluation results for the proposed flow. Finally we show the simplicity and expandability of EasyRouter with a three-dimensional (3D) FPGA case study. Conclusions are given in Section 6.

2. Related Works

2.1 FPGA design CAD tools

Xilinx ISE and Altera Quartus are commercial CAD tools used to implement circuits on their FPGAs. On the other hand, open source design flows like Verilog-to-Routing (VTR) project [5] are used for academic FPGA researches. The VTR project consists of the placement and routing tool Versatile Packing, Placement and Routing (VPR) [11], the synthesis tool ODIN II [6], and technology mapping tool ABC [7]. VPR [11] is the CAD tool that directly related to the FPGA physical architecture.

Because VPR cannot be used for unsupported architectures, many other FPGA design frameworks have been developed for various devices. Grant et al. [8] employed a typical FPGA design flow together with a new placing, routing, and scheduling tool for their coarse-grained architecture. Ababei et al. [9] and Miyamoto et al. [10] proposed design flows for a 3D-FPGA. The authors of [9] developed their TPR on the basis of VPR 4.0, while those of [10] used a modified VPR for 3D-FPGA.

2.2 Issues of traditional design flows

We now discuss two issues of VPR since it is directly related to the physical architecture of the FPGA.

First, the architecture-description-file based architecture definition method provides flexibility for various logic block structures. However, the flexibility of routing structure is still limited to the supported island style architectures. For much of our research, such as on a 3D-FPGA, we have to modify the VPR to implement various routing architectures. It consumes considerable development time to master, modify, and debug the C-coded VPR.

Second, the VPR is integrated with a simple delay model to facilitate timing-driven routing and post-routing timing analysis. The final timing report consists of the logic and routing delays, which are calculated in different ways. Therefore, although the relative values of VPR delay results can fairly evaluate FPGA architectures, the absolute value has low accuracy for synthesizable FPGA IP design, which requires an accurate entire chip static timing analysis (STA) with a standard cell library. Further, VPR does not provide any function that links FPGA design flow with commercial VLSI CADs.

3. EasyRouter

In this section, we introduce the proposed routing tool EasyRouter. Based on the similar routing and reporting functions of VPR, EasyRouter has some improved features. First, because we developed EasyRouter in C# language with full object-oriented programming coding style, the amount of code and complexity was reduced, making it easier to understand and modify. Owing to the benefits of the open-source Mono runtime environment, EasyRouter can be executed in most operating systems. Second, we developed a script-based architecture definition mechanism by considering the code file itself to be the architecture definition file. This mechanism offers users maximum flexibility in implementing new architectures. Finally, we developed HDL codes and bitstream generation functions to facilitate the evaluation of the designed FPGA using commercial VLSI CADs. The block diagram of EasyRouter is shown in Fig. 1. We now describe each of the blocks in detail.

3.1 RRGraph building block

The RRGraph describes the target FPGA architecture with routing resources (nodes) and their connection relationships [11]. We describe the RRGraph with a graph data structure, which is independent with any FPGA architecture. Each routing resource in the RRGraph is called an RRNode. The RRGraph is a collection of all necessary RRNodes.

As Fig. 1 shows, the RRGraph building block of EasyRouter reads the C# coded FPGA architecture script file

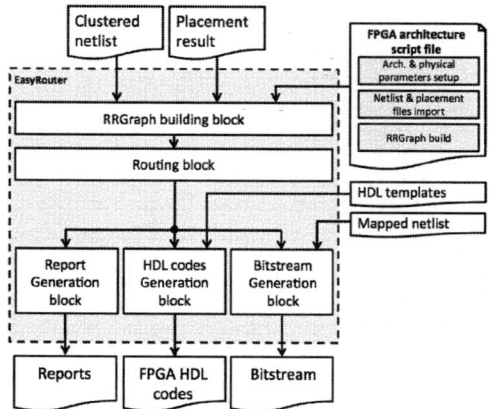

Fig. 1: EasyRouter block diagram.

to generate an RRGraph. The actual architectural dependent codes such as architecture and physical parameters setup, netlist and placement files import, and the RRGraph building are implemented in the RRGraph generation script files. The architecture and physical parameters setup block sets parameters of one FPGA architecture like the VPR architecture file does. New FPGA architecture can be implemented by modifying the RRGraph building codes of the script. The architecture script only returns architectural independent RRGraph to the routing block. The dynamic script support is implemented with the Dynamic Language Runtime (DLR) of the .net framework. With this feature, the FPGA architecture to be evaluated by EasyRouter can be changed by switching the RRGraph generation script input file. Therefore, new FPGA architecture can be implemented easily using the EasyRouter. And the architecture script is generic to implement various FPGA architectures. When evaluating many architectures, it is easy to switch between them without recompiling the main EasyRouter program.

3.2 Routing block

EasyRouter implements conventional breadth-first and timing-driven pathfinder routing algorithms [11]. Note that the timing-driven algorithm can improve delay of routing result when implementing customer circuits, however, it is not employed during the FPGA scale exploration phase because accurate physical delay information is unknown before the architecture implementation.

3.3 HDL codes and bitstream generation block

We developed EasyRouter using FPGA HDL codes and the user circuit configuration bitstream generation functions to link the academic FPGA design flow with the commercial VLSI CAD tools, since the routing algorithm stores a large amount of architecture information that can be used to generate HDL codes and bitstreams. As Fig. 3 shows, when

EasyRouter operates in the evaluation mode, the channel width (CW) and array size, which are input parameters, are fixed. Using the netlist file, placement result file, HDL codes templates, and architecture parameters, EasyRouter can generate all the FPGA HDL codes and an application bitstream.

First, we introduce HDL code generation. The logic part contains three levels of codes: the logic cell, basic logic element (BLE), and logic cluster (with a local connection block). For most FPGA architectures, these structures are homogeneous for all reconfigurable tiles. Therefore, the logic components of HDL codes can easily be prepared manually. The routing components of HDL codes are generated automatically with simple templates. The template consists of the structure of the switch box (SB), connection block (CB), and I/O block (IOB). The final routing HDL codes are generated according to the channel width and other routing parameters such as Fc_in, Fc_out and Fs [11]. Routing resources and their connections can be generated automatically according to the information maintained in the RRGraph of the router.

Next, we discuss bitstream generation. The logic element bitstream consists of the logic cell lookup table (LUT) and the configuration memory bit of the output multiplexer. The output multiplexer selects the output of the BLE directly from the LUT or through a register [11]. The logic element bitstream is generated according to the netlist after technology mapping. The routing bitstream contains configuration memory values of the SB, CB, local connection block (LCB), and IOB, which are generated according to the actual routing results.

3.4 Report generation block

The report generation block exports routed circuit information on the target device as the final execution stage of EasyRouter. The device array size, minimum channel width, the quantity of all routing resources, and the number of used routing resources are included in this exported report. These data are derived directly from a routed RRGraph, and are useful for device performance analysis.

In order to evaluating large devices efficiently or special VLSI technology (such as 3D-VLSI) that cannot be implemented easily, a fast performance analysis method of EasyRouter can be used. Because common FPGAs are composed of tiles of the same structure, area and delay performance can be calculated from the physical information of one FPGA tile. We first finish the layout of a tile structure with VLSI design flow and obtain its area. Then the device area can be obtained from the product of the tile area and $ArraySize \times ArraySize$. We then perform timing analysis using a simplified tile delay model, which extracts some representative paths such as SB to SB, Channel to LB, and BLE input to output, and set their delay to values according to tile STA results. The critical path and its delay are obtained from the timing analysis using the

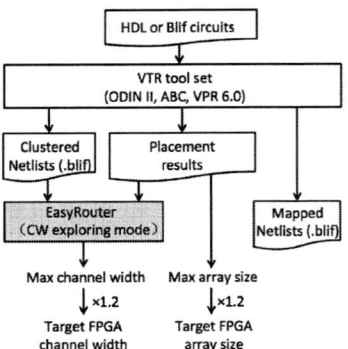

Fig. 2: Proposed framework: FPGA scale exploration.

routed RRGraph and these represent delays of the paths. The area and delay performance analysis at this stage is less accurate. However, it is fast and has sufficient precision for architecture exploration. We will prove this in Section 5.3.

4. Proposed FPGA IP Design Flow

Conventional FPGA architecture exploration and implementation processes involve two separate flows. The FPGA architecture is determined by academic FPGA design flow. However, in the implementation phase, commercial VLSI design flow are used which gives rise to two problems. One is that the academic design flow cannot provide high accuracy area, delay and power estimates. The other is that if design defects are found in the VLSI design phase, then it is necessary to restart from the FPGA design flow and a large number of HDL codes needs to be revised.

We propose an FPGA IP design flow that combines the FPGA and VLSI design flows, to solve the above problems. The proposed FPGA IP design flow consists of three parts: the conventional FPGA design flow, VLSI back-end design and analysis flow, and the novel tool EasyRouter which can bridge the two flows. By employing the proposed IP design flow, architecture exploration and implementation can be performed with high accuracy and within a reasonable execution time.

4.1 FPGA scale exploration

Since the FPGA IP core has limited on-chip area, FPGA scale exploration is necessary. The objective of FPGA scale exploration is to find a rational FPGA tile array size and routing channel width by implementing target application circuits.

Figure 2 shows how we link EasyRouter with VTR to perform FPGA scale exploration. The synthesis tool ODIN II reads and optimizes an HDL-described application circuit. The output of ODIN II is a Blif netlist as it is the standard format used to pass circuit information between academic FPGA tools. Blif format circuits (ex. MCNC benchmarks)

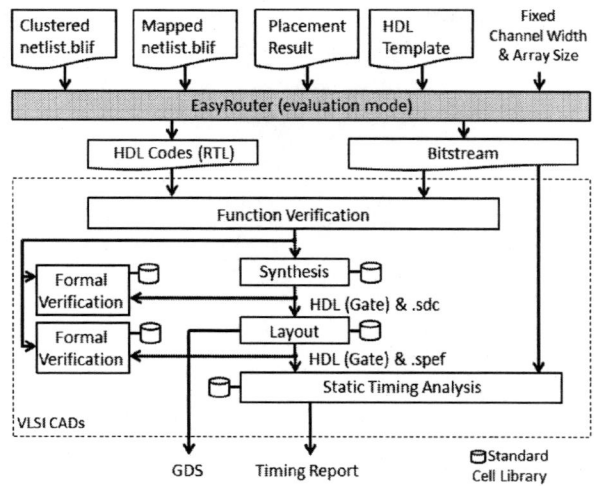

Fig. 3: Proposed framework: FPGA implementation.

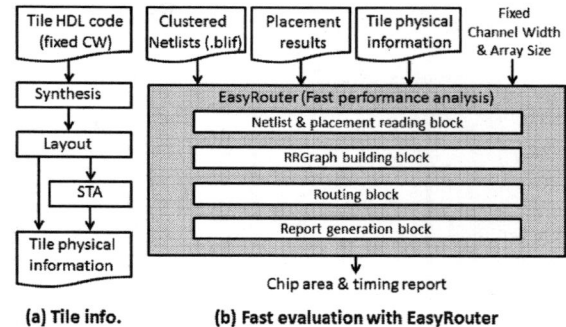

(a) Tile info.   **(b) Fast evaluation with EasyRouter**

Fig. 4: Proposed framework: Fast performance analysis.

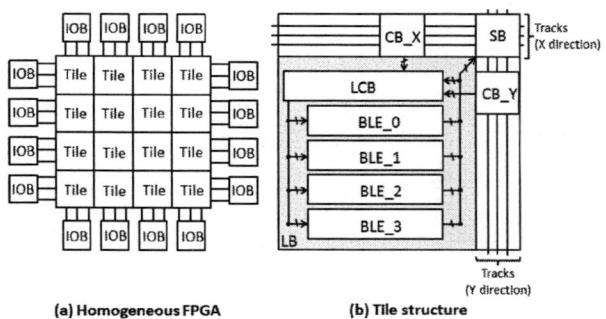

(a) Homogeneous FPGA   **(b) Tile structure**

Fig. 5: Homogeneous FPGA architecture.

can be directly inputted into ABC. The technology mapping tool ABC maps the netlist logic circuits into FPGA logic elements, which are typically k-input LUTs. In the case of VPR 6.0, the logic elements are first packed into clusters. The clustered logic blocks are then placed in an $n \times n$ tile array. Finally, we use EasyRouter to make the connections for the I/O pins of all logic blocks and I/O ports of the FPGA IP. Placement and routing are performed ten times for each circuit since different seeds (from 0 to 9) of the simulated annealing based placement algorithm generate different placement solutions. The routing result for each circuit is the average of the results of ten placement seeds.

4.2 FPGA IP implementation and performance analysis with commercial VLSI CADs

After the architecture is determined, we run EasyRouter in the evaluation mode to generate the FPGA HDL codes and each circuit's bitstream, which is shown in Fig. 3. When all the FPGA HDL codes and an application bitstream are generated, we can start the back-end design with commercial VLSI design CAD tools. Back-end design flows differ according to the technique used and the researcher's design experience. However, in general, the steps shown in Fig. 3 are necessary, which are the same with common ASIC design flow.

4.3 Fast performance analysis with EasyRouter

The full back-end design of a large scale FPGA device is an intensely time consuming process. On the other hand, special VLSI process devices such as the 3D-FPGA cannot presently be implemented easily because of the lack of available CADs support and process technology. For these reasons, the evaluation flow presented in Fig. 3 is sometimes not efficient or not applicable. Therefore, we developed a fast

performance analysis function for EasyRouter to evaluate these devices.

Fig. 4 shows the flow when using EasyRouter for fast performance analysis. When the target device architecture is determined with the method described in Section 4.1, we can make HDL code for one tile of the target device. We then implement the one tile HDL code with VLSI design flow and obtain the physical information such as area and delays of representative paths, as shown in Fig. 4 (a). Finally, as shown in Fig. 4 (b), in the fast performance analysis mode with this physical information, EasyRouter executes the area reports and timing results.

5. Evaluation

In this section, we first introduce the evaluation conditions. Second, we report the performance of EasyRouter, which include the execution time and minimum channel width for each benchmark. We then evaluate the proposed post-routing performance evaluation flow with a homogeneous FPGA IP. Finally, we show the expandability of EasyRouter with a 3D-FPGA case study.

5.1 Evaluation conditions

During the EasyRouter performance evaluations, we used conventional island style FPGA that supported by VPR

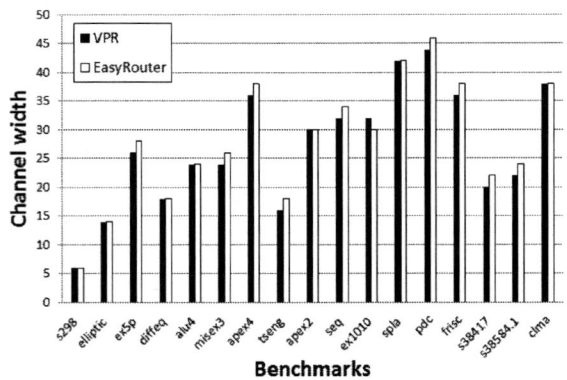

Fig. 6: Island style FPGA channel widths.

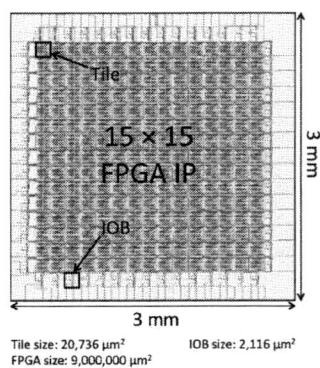

Fig. 7: FPGA IP layout.

[11]. For post-routing performance evaluation and 3D-FPGA case study, we employed a novel homogeneous FPGA architecture [12], as shown in Fig. 5. In this device, all tiles have the same structure, unlike the island-style FPGA architecture, which is composed of several types of different tiles. Therefore, the homogeneous FPGA architecture can be easily produced and tested. The details and performance of this architecture have been described in a previous paper [12]. In this evaluation we employed 4-LUT with cluster size of four. The number of inputs of LB was ten. The SB was wilton type. The Fs value was 3 and the Fc value was 0.5.

Circuits from the largest 20 MCNC benchmark were used for evaluation. The device was designed using e-Shuttle 65 nm CMOS technology. The functional simulation tool was ModelSim 6.5b. The design was synthesized with Synopsys Design Compiler F-2011.09-SP2. The layout was performed using Cadence EDI system 10.13. We checked the gate level netlists outputted from the Design Compiler and EDI with Formality A-2008.03-SP3. Finally, the STA was performed with PrimeTime F-2011.12-SP1.

For the comparison, the area and delay physical parameters of VPR were derived in the same flow and technology process. A tile of the target FPGA was synthesized and layouted with the same back-end design flow. The tile area was derived from the GDS after layout. Delays within the LB were extracted with the STA. The wire RC model was analyzed with the HSpice. All physical parameters were written into the architecture file in the VPR format. Note that out evaluation targets of this evaluation were synthesizalbe FPGAs. The evaluation result of VPR may be different for full-custom designed FPGA.

5.2 EasyRouter performance evaluation

As we talked, the most time-consuming function of a router is the heap sort. We tested the same heap sort algorithm in C and C#. The basic test operation involves adding numbers from 0 to 999,999 to a min-heap and then deleting it to empty from the top. The basic test operation was repeated for 30 times. Then we compared the execution time for the two implementations. The results showed that the C# implementation was around 5.0 times slower than the C implementation, because of the performance difference of C# and C language. This implies that when implementing a given routing algorithm, the C# program will be at least 5.0 times slower than the C program.

We evaluated the execution time of 17 benchmarks. According to the results, EasyRouter was 8.4 times slower than VPR on average. However, for large circuits like frisk, pdc, and clma, EasyRouter was near to 5.0 times slower. This is because for large circuits, the heap sort operations dominate the execution time to a greater extent. We examined the s298, alu4, and pdc circuits, and the cpu instruction sampling results showed that the execution time ratio of the heap function were 65.8%, 76.1%, and 83.2%. Therefore, for large circuits, the execution time overhead of EasyRouter was close to the performance difference between the C and C# implementations.

Fig. 6 shows the minimum channel widths of EasyRouter and VPR. We can see that the routing performance of both tools were similar. A reason the channel width of both differ in some circuits, is that during the RRGraph searching step, the expansion order of the RRNode with the same cost value will influence the routing results. However, because of this, the influence of the minimum channel width was only about a factor of two (the minimum change step for unidirectional routing architecture). Therefore, EasyRouter has a capability that is almost identical to that of VPR.

5.3 Post-routing performance evaluation

Because the FPGA IP designs have limited die size, we used a device array size of 15×15 to introduce the generation of HDL codes and bitstreams, and post-routing evaluation methods. The CW was fixed to 50. We selected the six circuits from the 20 largest MCNC benchmarks to evaluate the target device, because they can be implemented with a

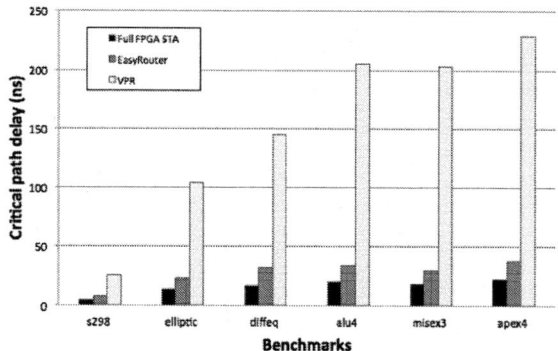

Fig. 8: Delay results.

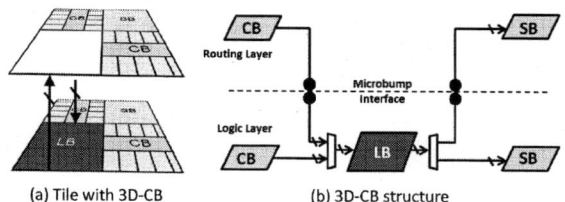

(a) Tile with 3D-CB   (b) 3D-CB structure

Fig. 9: Target 3D-FPGA architecture.

target device of array size of 15×15.

The area calculation model of VPR multiplies the area of one tile by the number of tiles in the array. With an accurate tile area after layout, this module is reliable. Therefore, we only provided the physical area information of the designed target device, which is presented in Fig. 7.

Fig. 8 shows the critical path delay calculated by the flow of EasyRouter with full FPGA VLSI back-end design and STA (Full FPGA STA), EasyRouter fast performance analysis (EasyRouter), and VPR. We believe the critical path delay of the full FPGA STA was an accurate delay value because the evaluation of commercial VLSI design flow with a standard cell library has the highest simulation accuracy in industry. Note that we used the breadth-first router of EasyRouter and VPR for pure delay accuracy comparison.

The delay value accuracy calculated by VPR was 8.9 times lower than that obtained from the full FPGA STA on average. This was because the delay model of VPR was pessimistic and had low accuracy. For example, all routing segment delays were calculated with the same wire RC model. In an actual final layout, the placement was optimized and the physical delays were different. However, we can see that VPR correctly reflected the performance relationship between the circuits. This shows the reliability of VPR as a fast architecture exploration tool.

The result accuracy calculated by EasyRouter fast performance analysis was 1.7 times lower than that obtained from the full FPGA STA on average. This result showed that EasyRouter improved delay accuracy 5.1 times than VPR on average. This was because, although EasyRouter used a similar pessimistic model as VPR, all representative path delays were calculated with the high accuracy STA process. On the other hand, the routing delay and logic delay of VPR was calculated with different models. Therefore, we conclude that the EasyRouter fast performance analysis method is reliable for fast high accuracy device evaluation.

5.4 3D-FPGA case study

EasyRouter is designed to implement new FPGA architectures easily. In this section, we show the expandability of EasyRouter by evaluating a novel 3D-FPGA architecture that was developed in a previous work [13]. The area and critical path delay performance of the homogeneous 2D-FPGA and the novel 3D-FPGA were compared. The new 3D-FPGA architecture script file was modified from a conventional 2D-FPGA architecture script file by adding only few codes for vertical connections of 3D-VLSI technology.

5.4.1 Target 3D-FPGA architecture

Fig. 9(a) and (b) shows the tile image and the detail of the proposed 3D routing architectures. The two layers in the proposed 3D-FPGA were the logic and routing layers. We employed the face-down 3D stacking technique to connect two dies with micro bumps. The tiles on the logic layer had a LB and a small part of the routing resources, while the tiles on the routing layer had only routing resources. The tiles for the two layers were designed within approximately the same area. Different from conventional 3D routing architectures with 3D-SBs, we made the 3D connections on the input and output pins of the LB, which we named 3D-CB structure. The router chose one net to be routed on either the logic layer or the routing layer.

By dividing routing resources into two layers, we achieved a smaller tile. A smaller tile means a higher logic density, shorter routing wire, and faster signal transportation. Therefore, the routing performance could be improved. Moreover, the proposed 3D-FPGA was realistic, because the number of inter-layer connections within one tile was equal to the number of input and output pins of the LB. Compared to conventional the 3D-FPGA based on the 3D-SB, which required two times the number of channel width inter-layer connections, the proposed architecture significantly reduced the requirement for inter-layer connections.

5.4.2 Evaluation conditions and results

We successfully implemented the 3D-FPGA architecture on EasyRouter in a relatively short development time. The FPGA scale exploration was performed with the flow that we introduced in Section 4.1. The performance analysis was performed using the method that we described in Section

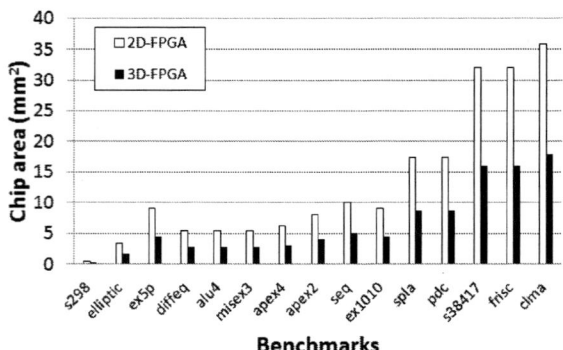

Fig. 10: Area result for 3D-FPGA.

4.3. We simply define the delay of one vertical connection between logic layer and routing layer as the same delay of one segment wire.

Fig. 10 shows the evaluation results for the area. We can see that the proposed 3D-FPGA used half the package area of 2D-FPGA by allocating nets on two layers. This means the logic density had improved by about a factor of two. The critical path delay also improved about 4% on average. This is because the increased channel width has better routability, and the smaller tile has shorter routing wire length.

With this 3D-FPGA case study, we can say various architectures can be implemented on the EasyRouter framework within a relatively short development time. High accuracy area and delay performance analysis can also be performed with the proposed framework.

6. Conclusions

In this paper, we proposed a novel FPGA routing tool, EasyRouter, and an FPGA IP design flow that combines conventional FPGA design tools with VLSI CADs. Easy-Router facilitates easy modeling of new FPGA architectures without any limitations, which can significantly shorten the development cycle. EasyRouter can also automatically generate device HDL codes and configuration bitstream files of the implemented circuits that can be processed by VLSI CADs. With this design flow, accurate physical information STA can be reported when a new FPGA IP architecture is evaluated with reliable commercial VLSI CADs. For FPGA architectures that cannot be easily implemented with present VLSI process, EasyRouter provides a fast performance analysis flow, which improved delay accuracy 5.1 times than VPR on average. We have also evaluated the proposed FPGA design flow with three different devices to show its performance and expandability.

References

[1] I. Kuon, A. Egier, and J. Rose, "Design, layout and verification of an FPGA using automated tools," Proc. of the 2005 ACM/SIGDA International Symposium on Field Programmable Gate Arrays, pp.215-226, Feb. 2005.

[2] "Zynq All Programmable SoC Architecture," 2012. http://www.xilinx.com/products/silicon-devices/soc/index.htm.

[3] "SoC FPGAs: Integration to Reduce Power, Cost, and Board Size," 2012. http://www.altera.com/devices/processor/soc-fpga/proc-soc-fpga.html.

[4] "eFPGA Core IP: The embedded Field Programmable Gate Array IP," 2012. http://www.menta.fr/down/ProductBrief_eFPGA_Core.pdf.

[5] J. Rose, J. Luu, C. W. Yu, O. Densmore, J. Goeders, A. Somerville, K. B. Kent, P. Jamieson, and J. Anderson, "The VTR Project: Architecture and CAD for FPGAs from Verilog to Routing," Proc. of the 2012 ACM/SIGDA International Symposium on Field Programmable Gate Arrays, pp.77-86, Feb. 2012.

[6] P. Jamieson, K. Kent, F. Gharibian, and L. Shannon, "Odin II-An Open-Source Verilog HDL Synthesis Tool for CAD Research," IEEE Annual International Symposium on Field programmable Custom Computing Machines, pp.149-156, May 2010.

[7] A. Mishchenko et al., "ABC: A System for Sequential Synthesis and Verification," http://www.eecs.berkeley.edu/ alanmi/abc/, 2009.

[8] D. Grant, C. Wang, and G. G. F. Lemieux, "A CAD Framework for MALIBU: An FPGA with Time-multiplexed Coarse-grained Elements," Proc. of the 2011 ACM/SIGDA International Symposium on Field Programmable Gate Arrays, pp.77-86, Feb. 2011.

[9] C. Ababei, H. Mogal, and K. Bazargan, "Three-dimensional Place and Route for FPGAs," IEEE Tran. on Computer Aided Design of Integrated Circuits and Systems, pp.1132-1140, Jun. 2006.

[10] N. Miyamoto, Y. Matsumoto, H. Koike, T. Matsumura, K. Osada, Y. Nakagawa, and T. Ohmi, "Development of a CAD Tool for 3D-FPGAs," Proc. of the 2010 3D Systems Integration Conference, pp.1-6, Nov. 2010.

[11] V. Betz, J. Rose, and A. Marquardt, "Architecture and CAD for Deep-Submicron FPGAs," Kluwer Academic Publishers, Mar. 1999.

[12] K. Inoue, M. Koga, M.Iida, M. Amagasaki, Y. Ichida, M. Saji, J. Iida, and T. Sueyoshi, "An Easily Testable Routing Architecture and Prototype Chip," IEICE Trans. Inf. & Syst., vol. E95-D, oo.303-313, Feb. 2012.

[13] Q. Zhao, Y. Iwai, M. Amagasaki, Y. Ichida, M. Saji, J. Iida, and T. Sueyoshi, "A Novel Reconfigurable Logic Device Base on 3D Stack Technology," Proc. Of the 3D Systems Integration Conference, P-2-14, Feb. 2012.

Types, signatures, interfaces, and components in NOOP:
The core of an adaptive run-time

Anders Andersen
Department of Computer Science
Faculty of Science and Technology
University of Tromsø
9037 Tromsø, Norway

Abstract— *Python is a dynamic language well suited to build a run-time providing adaptive support to distributed applications. NOOP introduces a type language and a way to apply typing to functions (and methods). This type system is described in the first part of this paper. The second part use this type system to create interfaces and a software component model. And finally it is discussed how NOOP can provide adaptive support to distributed applications.*

Keywords: Software components, Adaptive, Typing, Python.

1. Introduction

Python is a dynamic interpreted language with implicit typing. When a new function is defined no explicit type information is provided. Argument values are assigned values at call time based on their position or name. It is possible for arguments to have a default value. It is also possible to combine positional and named arguments when a function call is performed. A typical usage of this is to have one or two obligatory positional arguments followed by a set of named optional arguments.

The `withdraw` function in Figure 1 has two obligatory positional arguments `account` and `amount` and two optional named arguments `on_behalf_of` and `message`. At call time in this example three of these arguments are provided values, and therefore implicit given a type. The two optional arguments were at define time given a default value and therefore an implicit type. However, in Python any argument (and any variable) can be assigned a value of different type everytime it is used (sometimes this is intentional).

In large software projects well-defined function behavior is important. Part of this is well-defined arguments and return values. Introduction of types and a type system is a common approach to support this. If this is introduced for Python functions the actual implementation of these functions can be made less complex and less error prone. The reason is that the programmer can expect that the arguments are of the correct type. In a distributed setting this can be extended to avoid that a remote method invocation is performed if the correct type of arguments are not provided. Raising such an error locally at the callee is more efficient.

The type of arguments and return values of a function is the signature of the function. If functions are class methods we can call the set of signatures provide by the class instances for the interface. If all interaction of a class instance (or an object) is through well-defined interfaces this is close to what commonly is called a software component [1].

Python does not have type safe functions, but Python provides the necessary mechanisms to implement it. In the NOOP project a type system for Python functions that makes it possible to define the signature of such functions has been implemented. We have chosen a hybrid approach to the NOOP type system [2] where it is possible to combine statical typing of NOOP with the dynamic typing of Python. Signatures can be used to create interfaces. Interfaces applied to well-defined Python classes are the core of NOOP software components. Such components can be deployed in a NOOP run-time both as single component or as a composition of components. At deploy time a contract between the component and the run-time is provided. This contract includes the requirements of the component that has to be fulfilled by the run-time. How the contract is fulfilled also depends on the given context of the deployed component.

In this paper will present the type system of NOOP, how this is used to define the signature of Python functions, and how such signatures are used to define interfaces. NOOP components and the deployment of such components will be introduced. Finally, its is discussed how NOOP can provide adaptive support to distributed applications. A more detailed overview of NOOP is available in [3].

2. Types and signatures

Python provides a set of built-in types. For example, `type(1)` is `int`. In NOOP the type system has been extended with composite types. A few examples are given in Figure 2. The first example gives us the possibility to define a tuple with a well-defined number of elements with well-defined types (a tuple with three elements of the type `int`, `str`, and `float`). The second example gives us the possibility to define a list of integers (lists in Python can have any combination of value types). The third example gives us the possibility to define a dictionary of any length where the keys are of type `str` and the values are of type `int`. And the last example provides a dictionary with two elements where the first key is `"id"` and the second key is `"sh"`, and the value of `"id"` is of type `int` and the value of `"sh"` is of type `str`.

A few new type constructors have been added to NOOP. The reason is that such constructors can be used to give a more precise definition of the programmer's intention. Figure 3 lists the new type constructors. The extended type system is available in the `signature` module.

All the type constructors are used to create new types. The `whatever` type is true for any values. The `opt` type says that the value should either be of this type or not present at all. The `one` type says that the value should be of one of the listed types. The type constructor `pred` has an argument `p` that is a predicate. This predicate is a function that accepts one argument and returns either `True` or `False`. The argument is the value of the applied argument to the type. The `tgtz` type below specifies all integers larger than zero:

```
def gtz(): return v > 0
```

```
def withdraw(account, amount, on_behalf_of="", message=""):      1
    # The actual implementation is ignored in this example        2
    return amount                                                 3
new_balance = withdraw(13219254, 125.25, message="School trip")   4
```

Fig. 1: Python function combining positional and named arguments.

```
type((1, "foo", 2.3))        is (int, str, float)
type([1, 4, 7, 8])           is [int]
type({"ID": 212, "GID": 100}) is {str: int}
type({"id": 42, "sh": "bash"}) is {"id": int, "sh": str}
```

Fig. 2: Composite types in NOOP.

whatever	Value of any type
opt(t)	Value of type t or no value
one(t_1, t_2, ..., t_n)	Value of either type t_1, t_2, ...
pred(t,p)	Value of the type t and p is true

Fig. 3: New type constructors in NOOP.

```
tgtz = pred(int, gtz)
```

The predicate type constructor is used to limit the accepted values of a given type. It should not be confused with the concept of dependent types [4], [5] that can create more expressive type constructors. Currently NOOP does not provide such type constructors.

The type system in NOOP is extensible. It is easy to create new types using the type constructors discussed above. It is also possible to create completely new types constructors using the typespec class. Create a new class that inherits the typespec class and implement the actual type check for the new type in the __call__ method. If the new type constructor is parameterized the __init__ method has to be implemented too. The whatever type is not parameterized, but the other type constructors listed in Figure 3 are. A new parameterized type constructor for positive integers up to a given value is implemented in Figure 4. The __init__ method is called when a new type is created using the type constructor (line 10). The __call__ method should have exactly one argument. This is the value that is type checked against the type when NOOP performs type checking. The __call__ method should raise a SignatureError if the value does not match the type.

In NOOP, two approaches are used to add signatures to functions. The first approach use Python decorators (available for functions since Python 2.4). Decorators can be applied to Python functions by a line starting with @ before the function definition. Following the @ is the name of the decorator and optionally a set of arguments. A Python decorator is implemented as a function. In NOOP a signature decorator can be used to add signatures to functions. The @signature decorator takes three arguments.

```
class maxint(typespec):                    2
    def __init__(self, max):               3
        self.max = max                     4
    def __call__(self, value=missing):     5
        if ((not type(value) is int) or    6
            (value < 0) or                 7
            (value > self.max)):           8
            raise SignatureError("No match") 9
```

Fig. 4: A new type constructor maxint.

The first argument is the type specification of the decorated function's arguments. It is either a tuple or a dictionary. Each element of the tuple or the dictionary represents an argument to the function. If it is a dictionary the type specification is given using the names of the arguments. The arguments of the withdraw function above could be specified like this (the first line as a tuple and the following lines as a dictionary):

```
(int, float, opt(str), opt(str))       1
{"account": int, "amount": float,      2
 "on_behalf_of": opt(str),             3
 "message": opt(str)}                  4
```

The second argument of the @signature decorator is the type specification of the decorated function's return value. This is just the return value type. The return value type of the withdraw function above is float. The third argument is a list of exceptions the decorated function might raise during its execution. If the withdraw function above raised an IndexError when an unknown account number was applied the exception list could be specified with [IndexError]. The complete signature of the withdraw function using the @signature decorator is shown in Figure 5.

It is also possible to specify the @signature decorator with named arguments. The arguments type specification in named args, the return value type specification is named ret, and the list of exceptions is named exc. This is a signature with named arguments for the gtz function:

```
@signature(args=(int,), ret=bool,      2
           exc=[TypeError])            3
def gtz(v):                            4
    return v > 0                       5
```

The second approach to add signatures to Python functions in NOOP is to use annotations. Annotations has been available since Python 3.0. In NOOP we use annotations to annotate arguments and return values of functions with types. When a function is defined each argument can be annotated using a colon. If a function has an argument s of type str, the argument can be annotated like this: s: str. To specify the type of the return value of a function the function is annotated using ->. To apply the possible list of exceptions a function can raise we still have to use the @signature decorator.

At define time the function is analyzed to see if it matches the type specification. At call time type checking ensures that no arguments not matching the type specification is forwarded to the function. Type checking also ensures that the return value matches the type specification and that no exception not defined in the signature is raised. If either of these fails a SignatureError exception is raised.

It is possible to completely ignore exceptions in type checking at call time. The consequence is that *any* exceptions raised by the function will be thrown back to the caller. To achieve this effect the exception paramater (exc) of the @signature decorator is set to None This can also be achieved by providing no value for this argument.

```
@signature(((int,float,opt(str),opt(str)), float, [IndexError])        2
def withdraw(account, amount, on_behalf_of="", message=""):            3
    # The actual implementation is ignored in this example            4
    return amount                                                     5
```

Fig. 5: Signature decorator for the `withdraw` function.

```
mSig = ((int, int), int, [])        1
iMath = {"add": mSig, "sub": mSig}  2

@interfaces(math=iMath)             4
class Math:                         5
    def add(self, x:int, y:int) -> int:    6
        return x + y                7
    def sub(self, x:int, y:int) -> int:    8
        return x - y                9
```

Fig. 6: A `Math` class with an interface `math`.

```
@receptacles(m=iMath)               4
class Wallet:                       5
    def __init__(self):             6
        self.v = 0                  7
    def doSave(self, x: int):       8
        self.v = m.add(self.v, x)   9
    def doSpend(self, x: int):      10
        self.v = m.sub(self.v, x)   11
```

Fig. 7: A `Wallet` class with a receptacle m.

```
mSig = ((int, int), int, [])        1
iMath = {"add": mSig, "sub": mSig}  2

@component(provides={"math": iMath})  4
class Math:                         5
    def add(self, x:int, y:int) -> int:    6
        return x + y                7
    def sub(self, x:int, y:int) -> int:    8
        return x - y                9
```

Fig. 8: A `Math` component providing interface `math`.

receptacle can be bound to such an interface. The `@receptacles` decorator is used to add receptacles to an object. In Figure 7 the receptacle m is added to all objects of the `Wallet` class. The receptacle m can then be used to call to methods of an interface of the type `iMath` (like the `math` interface of `Math` objects). Before m can be used it has to be bound to an interface of type `iMath`. The following code makes an instance of both the `Math` and `Wallet` class, connects the receptacle m of the wallet to the math object, and perform the `doSave` operation of the wallet object. The `doSave` operation accesses the `add` method of the math object though the receptacle m and the interface `math`.

```
myWallet = Wallet()                            3
myMath = Math()                                4
localBind(myMath["math"],myWallet["m"])        5
myWallet.doSave(145)                           6
```

3. Interfaces and receptacles

The NOOP approach to interfaces differs a lot from the now rejected proposal for Python found in PEP 245 [6]. PEP 245 proposes interfaces similar to what is found in Java where a class implements a defined interface. This is also true for Zope interfaces [7]. While the NOOP approach also can be used like this, its main purpose is to support the interaction between objects. In that sense it is closer to interfaces related to software components or remote invocation.

In NOOP interfaces of objects lists methods with signatures. One object can implement several interfaces. Receptacles represent interfaces used by objects. Object implementations refer to external interfaces through receptacles and receptacles are explicit bound to interfaces (late binding). The binding operation (e.g. `bind`) can be (and often is) performed outside the object implementation.

The `@interface` decorator is used to create interfaces on a Python object in NOOP. To the interface decorator named arguments are applied. The names represents the name of the interface. The value list the methods and their signatures. A `Math` class that can be used to create objects with an interface `math` of type `iMath` with two metods `add` and `sub` are defined in Figure 6 (`mSig` is the signature of both method `add` and `sub`). The signature of each method specified in the `math` interface are applied to the matching methods of the class. It is possible apply these signatures explicit to each method in the class. Type checking will then ensure that the signatures of the methods match the signatures of the interface. In the example in Figure 6 the methods are annotated with the type information.

If an object should access an interface of another object receptacles are used. A receptacle refers to an external interface implementation that is unknown at definition time. Later, this

4. Software components

A NOOP component is a Python object with well defined external behavior defined by a set of interfaces (`provides`), a set of receptacles (`uses`), and a run-time contract. To implement a NOOP component a `@component` decorator is added to the class of the object. It is easy to rebrand the `Math` and `Wallet` class to NOOP components. The `@interfaces` and `@receptacles` decorators are replaced with `@component` decorators that include the named arguments `provides` and `uses`. The `provides` argument lists the interfaces provided by this component, and the `uses` argument lists the interfaces used by this component (the receptacles). Figure 8 and 9 show the implementation of the `Math` component and the `Wallet` component, respectively. In the `Wallet` component we have added a provided interface `wallet`.

A NOOP component is not instantiated like ordinary Python objects. A NOOP component is deployed, and the run-time contract is applied to the component at deploy time. The run-time contract includes external interfaces used by the component and life-cycle management information.

The deployment operation returns a unique reference for the component. This reference is a global unique reference that can be used to refer to this component globally in any NOOP run-time. Every NOOP run-time (in NOOP called a capsule) has to implement a deploy method. The actual implementation might

```
wSig = ((int,), None, [])                 1
cSig = ((), int, [])                      2
iWallet = {"doSave":wSig, "doSpend":wSig, 3
           "content": cSig}               4

@component(provides={"wallet": iWallet},  5
           uses={"m": iMath})             6
class Wallet:                             7
    def __init__(self):                   8
        self.v = 0                        9
    def doSave(self, x: int):             10
        self.v = m.add(self.v, x)         11
    def doSpend(self, x: int):            12
        self.v = m.sub(self.v, x)         13
    def content(self):                    14
        return self.v                     15
```

Fig. 9: A `Wallet` component providing interface `wallet` and using interface `m`.

vary depending of the features and services provided by the run-time. The deploy-time contract can be used to specify features and services needed by a given component (or composition of components).

The simplest contract possible is an empty contract. In NOOP it is created as an empty dictionary:

```
contract = {}
```

A more common contract of a component maps its receptacles to external interfaces using the `bind` argument. For the `Wallet` component the deploy contract could be specified like this (`mathRef` is the unique reference to a `Math` component):

```
contract={"bind":{"m":mathRef["math"]}}
```

The contract specifies that a binding between the m receptacle of the `Wallet` and the `math` interface of the `Math` component has to be created. To complete the example of the `Math` and `Wallet` component, this is how we deploy and use a `Math` component and a `Wallet` component using an empty contract for the `Math` component and a simple `bind` contract for the `Wallet` component:

```
mathRef=deploy(Math,{})                       5
contract={"bind":{"m":mathRef["math"]}}       6
walletRef=deploy(Wallet,contract)             7
walletRef["wallet"].doSave(145)               8
```

In a NOOP run-time the component references can be used as proxies. The interfaces (and receptacles) can be accessed using their names as keys (like a Python dictionary). The methods of the interfaces can be accessed using ordinary dot-notation.

In NOOP a composite component is a composition of components. Every single component in the composition have an individual contract, and the composition of components have a common contract. All components of a composition is deployed in a single operation. The actual steps performed when a composition is deployed are these: (i) All components are instantiated. (ii) The contracts are applied to the components. (iii) The composition contract is applied to the composition.

Software components in NOOP are an unit for deployment. It is possible to see a component (and a composite component) as a unit that can be distributed independently and deployed in different applications and systems. The details of how this is achieved is out of the scope of this paper.

5. Dynamic support

Late binding and re-binding is an important part of the dynamic application support provided by NOOP. Components access other components, including system level components, through receptacles. Receptacles are bound to actual implementations at deploy time, and can be re-bound to other implementations later if this matches the given context better. Contracts specify the requirements of a component, including the services a component needs. Such contracts can include quality of service (QoS) specifications, and how a service is implemented might depend on the given context. Some services might be optional (a typical example is logging), and some contracts might specify a preferred service quality level and a minimum acceptable service quality level. The given context might also influence how the run-time fulfills the component requirements specified in the contract.

A typical NOOP application is a distributed application with a set of components deployed in a set of run-times called capsules. Each NOOP capsule an be tailored to the specific requirements of its deployed components. In NOOP the goal is not a single capsule type supporting a wide range of component requirements, but specialized capsules configured to support its deployed components (similar to the extensible application server discussed in [8]). A composite component might be distributed over several capsules. A typical example of such a distributed composite component is a remote binding that contains a stub and a skeleton deployed in different capsules.

When a component is deployed in a capsule the contract might specify complex requirements that includes adaption rules triggered by observed context changes. The details of such adaption is out of the scope of this paper. However, the NOOP component model, interfaces, receptacles and contracts are important mechanisms necessary to provide the adaptive run-time of NOOP.

6. Conclusion

The component model and the NOOP run-time is the base of several research projects investigating adaptive support for distributed applications. Different versions of the run-time exists, and the run-time itself can be configured to provide specialized support for a given type of application. The NOOP core functionality presented in this paper is used to investigate such adaptive and context sensitive behaviour further.

References

[1] C. Szyperski, *Component Software, Beyond Object-Oriented Programming*, 2nd ed., ser. The Component Software Series. Addison-Wesley, 2002.

[2] J. Siek and W. Taha, "Gradual typing for objects," in *Proceedings of the 21st European conference on Object-Oriented Programming: ECOOP 2007*. Springer-Verlag, 2007, pp. 2–27.

[3] A. Andersen, "The NOOP components and run-time described," University of Tromsø, Tech. Rep. 2013-73, 2013.

[4] J. McKinna, "Why dependent types matter," *ACM Sigplan Notices*, vol. 41, no. 1, pp. 1–1, Jan. 2006.

[5] H. Barendregt, "Lambda calculi with types," in *Handbook of Logic in Computer Science*, S. Abramsky, D. Gabbay, and T. Maibaum, Eds. Oxford Science Publications, 1992.

[6] M. Pelletier, *PEP 245: Python Interface Syntax*, 2001.

[7] B. Muthukadan, *A Comprehensive Guide to Zope Component Architecture*. Lulu, 2007.

[8] A. Munch-Ellingsen, D. P. Eriksen, and A. Andersen, "Argos, an extensible personal application server," in *Middleware 2007*, ser. Lecture Notes in Computer Science, vol. 4834, Nov. 2007, pp. 21–40.

Int'l Conf. Reconfigurable Systems and Algorithms | ERSA'13 |

47

Heterogeneous Multicore Platform with Accelerator Templates and Its Implementation on an FPGA with Hard-core CPUs

Yasuhiro Takei, Hasitha Muthumala Waidyasooriya, Masanori Hariyama and Michitaka Kameyama

Graduate School of Information Sciences, Tohoku University

Aoba 6-6-05, Aramaki, Aoba, Sendai, Miyagi, 980-8579, Japan

Email: {takei, hasitha, hariyama, kameyama}@ecei.tohoku.ac.jp

Abstract—*Heterogeneous multi-core architectures with CPUs and accelerators attract many attentions since they can achieve power-efficient computing in various areas from low-power embedded processing to high-performance computing. Since the optimal architecture is different from application to application, finding the most suitable accelerator is very important. In this paper, we propose an FPGA-based heterogeneous multi-core platform with custom accelerator templates. Accelerator templates can be reused after optimizing for different applications. According to the evaluation, the proposed platform gives comparable performance to the industrial heterogeneous multicore processors at around 1W of power.*

Keywords: Heterogeneous multicore processor, FPGA, Multimedia processing, High-performance-computing

1. Introduction

Applications used in low-power embedded processing to high performance computing have different tasks such as data-intensive tasks and control-intensive tasks. Therefore, optimal architecture is different from application to application. Heterogeneous multicore processing is proposed to execute applications power-efficiently. It uses different processor cores such as CPU cores and accelerator cores as shown in Fig.1. If the tasks of an application are correctly allocated to the most suitable processor cores, all the cores work together to increase the overall performances.

Examples of low-power heterogeneous multi-core processors are [1] and [2]. The former has multiple cores of CPUs and ALU arrays. The latter has multiple cores of CPUs, a micro-controller and SIMD (single-instruction multiple-data) type processors. Such commercially available processors are partially programmable so that a part of the data path and computations of processing elements (PEs) can be changed to some extent. However, due to the wide variety of tasks and their different memory requirements, this programmability is not enough to extract sufficient performance. Moreover, the programming environments in various heterogeneous architectures. Therefore, each time the architecture changes, large design time is required to re-map the application into the new architecture.

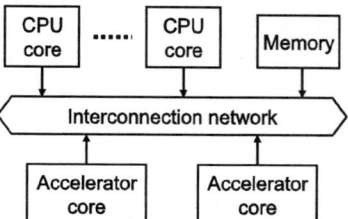

Fig. 1: Heterogeneous multi-core processor architecture

To solve these problems, we propose an FPGA-based platform for heterogeneous multicore processors to explore accelerator architectures suitable for applications. Recently, speed and power consumption of FPGAs are greatly improved, and it would be very practical to use the FPGA-based platform for real applications. The proposed platform consists of CPU cores suitable for control-intensive tasks and custom accelerator cores suitable for data-intensive tasks. The use of the architecture templates reduces the design effort to explore the architectures suitable for applications. It would also make it easy to re-use the same software on different accelerators derived from the same template. Moreover, the high reconfigurability of FPGAs enables to adopt the different types of accelerators for a single application depending on the nature of tasks. The major disadvantage of FPGA-based processors over the commercially available once is the low-performance of CPU cores since CPU cores are generated using look-up tables. Such "soft-core CPUs" cause large computation time and large data transfer time. However, recent FPGAs such as Xilinx Zynq and Altera Cyclone V contain "hard-core CPUs" operating at about 8 times faster than the soft-core CPUs.

This paper is an extension of the work done in [3] which explains the basic idea of the heterogeneous multicore platform. However, the soft-core CPU in [3] is replaced by a low-power hard-core CPU ("Cortex-A9 dual core ARM processor") using Xilinx Zynq so that the processing and data transfer time are significantly reduced. In this paper, as a typical architecture templates, we consider two types of custom accelerators: SIMD one-dimensional PE array (SIMD-1D) and MIMD two-dimensional PE array (MIMD-2D). The SIMD-1D accelerator is suitable for executing simple operations at a high degree of parallelism. The proposed

SIMD-1D accelerator is designed similar to the GPU data path to use the CUDA (compute unified devise architecture) [4] programming language. The MIMD-2D accelerator is suitable for executing complex operation at a medium degree of parallelism. To increase the memory access speed, we introduce a custom hardware called address generation unit (AGU). We can also reconfigure the data path, the number of PEs, the number of memory modules, and memory capacity according to the requirements of a given task to optimize the performance. The evaluation demonstrates that the proposed FPGA-based platform achieves good performance and low-power consumption comparable to industrial heterogeneous processors such as RP1 [1].

2. Heterogeneous multicore platform

2.1 Overall architecture

This section explains the architecture of the heterogeneous multi-core platform. Figure 2 shows the overall architecture. An external DDRII SDRAM is connected to the CPU core through the FPGA board. The custom accelerators have different architectures such as SIMD-1D and MIMD-2D.

It is important to reduce data-transfer time between cores for processing faster in heterogeneous multicore. In previous work [5], window-based image processing time and memory capacity are reduced by using optimal memory allocation and a data-transfer scheme. For further reduction the processing time, we overlap the data-transfer with data processing on different cores as shown in Fig.3. In FPGAs, We can determine the optimal number of accelerator cores and PEs so as to minimize the processing time.

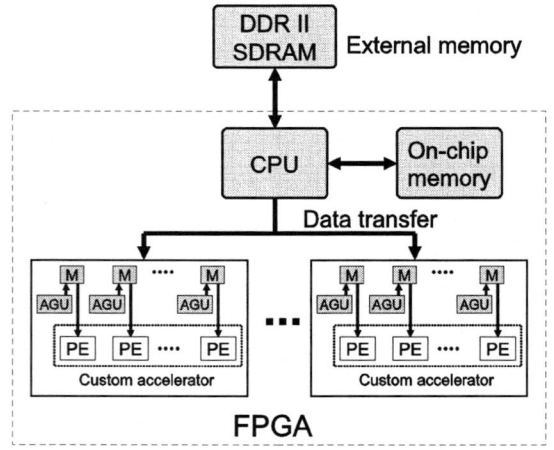

Fig. 2: Proposed heterogeneous multi-core architecture

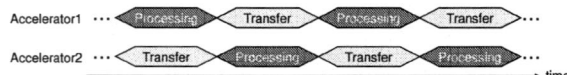

Fig. 3: Overlapping data-transfer and processing

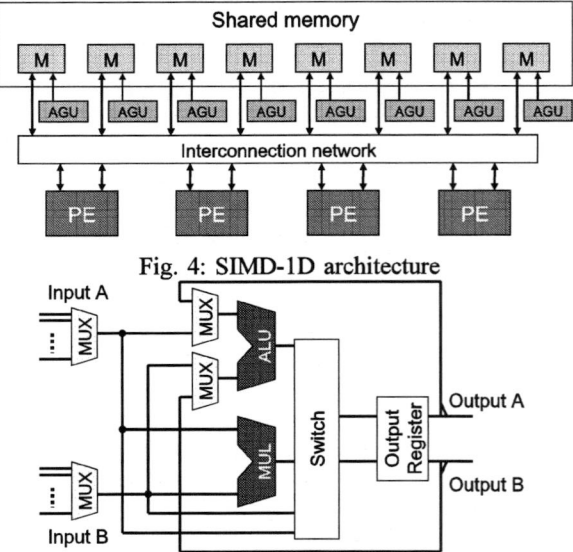

Fig. 4: SIMD-1D architecture

Fig. 5: Architecture of the PE

2.2 SIMD-1D accelerator

The proposed SIMD-1D accelerator is designed similar to the GPU accelerator so that we can use the same CUDA code. The basic idea of the SIMD-1D accelerator is discussed in [6]. It has a 1-dimensional array of PEs connected to the shared memory as shown in Fig.4. AGUs are included to increase the address generation speed. To execute an application, we have to divide it into independent threads where several of them can be executed in parallel. After the execution is finished, new threads are fed. When all the threads are executed, the resulting data are read by the CPU.

Figure 5 shows the architecture of a PE. It consists of a 16bit fixed-point ALU and a multiplier. Operations such as addition, accumulation subtraction, comparison and absolute difference computation are done in the ALU, and multiplication is done in the multiplier. Multiply-accumulation is done by a pipelining the multiplier and the adder.

In CPUs, the address calculation and data processing are done in the same ALU as shown in Fig.6(a). Therefore, when the addresses are calculated, we cannot do data processing. In the proposed architecture, the address calculation is done in the AGU shown in Fig.6(b). The address calculation and data processing are done in parallel so that we can reduce the total processing time. A detailed description about AGUs is given in [5]. As shown in Fig.2, accelerators in the proposed heterogeneous platform contain AGUs.

2.3 MIMD-2D accelerator

The proposed MIMD-2D accelerator is designed based on the FE-GA accelerator [1] that has a dynamically reconfigurable PE array. Figure 7 shows the proposed MIMD-2D accelerator. It consists of a 2-dimensional array of PEs,

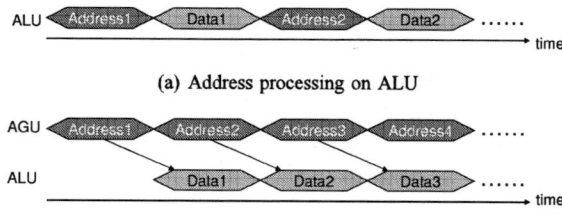

(a) Address processing on ALU

(b) Address processing on AGU

Fig. 6: Address processing

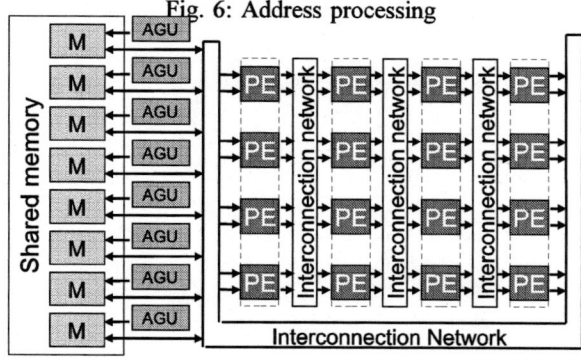

Fig. 7: MIMD-2D architecture model

local memory modules and AGUs. In order to simplify the interconnection network while still meeting the streaming applications, we limit the interconnection network; only leftmost PEs can directly retrieve data from local memory modules, and only rightmost PEs can directly write data to local memory modules. PEs, AGUs and interconnection network are dynamically reconfigurable. To implement applications, we have to divided it into multiple contexts that execute sequentially. Within a context, we can perform parallel computations. The computation starts after the configuration data of multiple contexts are written to the configuration memory of the accelerator. When the computation is finished, the resulting data are read by the CPU.

3. Evaluation

We implement the proposed heterogeneous multicore platform on Xilinx Zynq-7000 EPP ZC702 evaluation kit [7]. Since SIMD-1D and MIMD-2D architectures have different topologies, we perform two comparisons to evaluate the architectures. In the first comparison, the number of look-up-tables (LUTs) in both accelerators is a constant. In the second comparison, the degree of parallelism of the memory access is a constant. As shown in Table 1, SIMD9 and MIMD12 accelerators have almost the same number of LUTs. SIMD4 and MIMD12 accelerators have the same number of memory modules. Therefore, the degree of parallelism of the memory access is the same. In parallel processing, both the number PEs and the degree of parallelism with the memory are equally important.

We compare the processing time of filter computation and SAD-based template matching [8]. The image and window

Table 1: Specification of accelerator cores

Accelerator core	Number of PEs	Number of LUTs	Number of memories	Degree of parallelism
SIMD4	4×1	3301	8 (16kB)	4
SIMD9	9×1	7354	18 (18kB)	9
MIMD12	4×3	7322	8 (16kB)	4

sizes and the operating frequency are 256×16, 16×16 and 100MHz respectively. Table 2 shows the comparison of SIMD-1D (SIMD9) and MIMD-2D (MIMD12) accelerators when the number of LUTs is a constant. For the filter computation, the processing time of the SIMD-1D accelerator is less than half of that of the MIMD-2D accelerator. The SIMD-1D accelerator has a one-dimensional PE array, where all 9 PEs are directly connected to the memory as shown in Fig.4. The MIMD-2D architecture has a two-dimensional PE array of 4×3 where only leftmost 4 PEs can directly retrieve data from the local memory as shown in Fig.7. Therefore, the SIMD-1D accelerator has the higher degree of parallelism of memory access than the MIMD-2D accelerator. In the SAD computation, SIMD-1D accelerator is slightly faster than MIMD-2D accelerator. SAD computation requires two types of operations: absolute difference and addition. the MIMD-2D accelerator can perform these two operations at the same time by pipelining while SIMD-1D accelerator cannot. However, the processing time of the SIMD-1D accelerator is still smaller due to its high degree of parallelism. If we use an application that have three or more types of operations, the MIMD-2D accelerator could give much better results.

Table 2: Comparison 1 : The same number of LUTs

Application	Accelerator core	Processing time (ms)
Filter	SIMD9	0.069
	MIMD12	0.154
SAD	SIMD9	0.139
	MIMD12	0.154

Table 3 shows the comparison of SIMD-1D (SIMD4) and MIMD-2D (MIMD12) accelerators when the degree of parallelism of the memory access is a constant. In the filter computation, the processing times of the SIMD-1D and MIMD-2D accelerators are the same. This is because, multiplication and addition operations are pipelined in both accelerators, so that two operations are performed in one cycle. Moreover, both accelerators have the same degree of parallelism. In the SAD computation, the processing times in MIMD-2D accelerator is about half of that in SIMD-1D accelerator. As described above, the MIMD-2D accelerator can pipeline different type of operations (absolute difference and addition in SAD computation). Hence, MIMD-2D can obtain higher degree of parallelism of operations compared to the SIMD-1D accelerator under the condition of the same number of memory modules.

Let us compare the FPGA-based platform with conventional industrial heterogeneous multicore processors. Figure 8 shows the implemented architecture. There are MIMD-

Table 3: Comparison 2 : The same degree of parallelism

Application	Accelerator core	Processing time (ms)
Filter	SIMD4	0.156
	MIMD12	0.154
SAD	SIMD4	0.318
	MIMD12	0.154

2D accelerator cores which process the filter computation in parallel. Table 4 shows the resource utilization on the FPGA with four MIMD16 cores. Since the FPGA design tool removes unused units on the implemented architecture automatically, the resource utilization is smaller than expected. Note that the number of accelerator cores and the number of PEs in one core can be selected depending on the applications.

Table 5 shows the comparison of the filter computation time for the proposed FPGA-based platform and RP1 [1]. The image size is 640×480. The number of PEs on FPGA is 64, and it is equal to using two FE-GAs in RP1. When the number of FE-GA cores is two, the processing time on the proposed platform is very similar to that of RP1. The power consumption of both processors is around 1W. In conclusion, the FPGA-based heterogeneous multicore architecture provides comparable performance to the RP1 heterogeneous multicore processor.

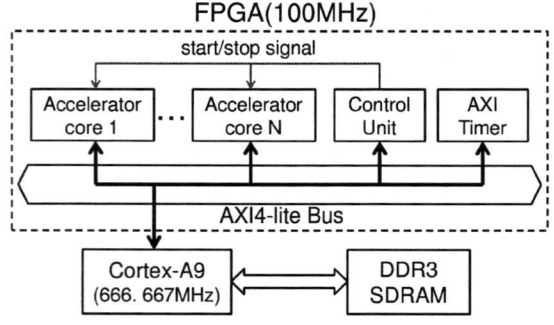

Fig. 8: Implemented architecture

Table 4: Resource utilization of four MIMD16 cores

Module	LUT	Register	Block RAM	DSP
Accelerators	1044	1604	18	16
Control unit	28	28	0	0
AXI timer	312	217	0	0
AXI Interconnect	397	182	0	0
Total	1781(3%)	2031(2%)	18(13%)	16(7%)

Table 5: Comparison of processing time

Window size	Processing time (ms)	
	Zynq 1xCortex-A9(666.667MHz) + FPGA(100MHz)	RP1 [5] 1xSH-4A(600MHz) + 2xFE-GA(300MHz)
12×12	46.51	36.24
18×18	70.50	72.94
24×24	115.89	96.55

4. Conclusion

We have proposed an FPGA-based heterogeneous multicore platform with custom accelerators. The accelerator cores are customizable for each application. Dedicated AGUs are used to increase the processing speed and to reduce the area and power. We evaluate the proposed platform using several examples and show that the proposed platform has performance comparable to industrial heterogeneous processors. To select the best accelerator for a given application, we have to match the requirements of the application with the properties of the accelerator under the design constraints. Most of the application requirements and accelerator properties can be parameterized and represented. The design constraints are the operating frequency, amount of hardware resources such as LUTs and memories, power consumption, etc. Our next step would be to find a relationship between those application requirements and the accelerator properties to satisfy the design constraints. Then we can automatically optimize the proposed heterogeneous platform for given applications.

Acknowledgment

This work is supported by MEXT KAKENHI Grant Number 12020735.

References

[1] H. Shikano, M. Ito, M. Onouchi, T. Todaka, T. Tsunoda, T. Kodama, K. Uchiyama, T. Odaka, T. Kamei, E. Nagahama, M. Kusaoke, Y. Nitta, Y. Wada, K. Kimura, H. Kasahara, "Heterogeneous Multi-Core Architecture That Enables 54x AAC-LC Stereo Encoding", *IEEE Journal of Solid-State Circuits*, Vol.43, No.4, pp.902-910, 2008.

[2] H. Kondo, M. Nakajima, N. Masui, S. Otani, N. Okumura, Y. Takata, T. Nasu, H. Takata, T. Higuchi, M. Sakugawa, H. Fujiwara, K. Ishida, K. Ishimi, S. Kaneko, T. Itoh, M. Sato, O. Yamamoto and K. Arimoto, "Design and Implementation of a Configurable Heterogeneous Multi-core SoC With Nine CPUs and Two Matrix Processors", *IEEE Journal of Solid-State Circuits*, Vol.43, No.4, pp.892-901, 2008.

[3] H. M. Waidyasooriya, Y. Takei, M. Hariyama and M. Kameyama, "FPGA implementation of Heterogeneous Multicore Platform with SIMD/MIMD Custom Accelerators", IEEE International Symposium on Circuits and Systems (ISCAS), pp.1339-1342, 2012.

[4] NVIDIA Corporation, "NVIDIA CUDA Programming Guide" Ver2.2.1, 2009.

[5] H. M. Waidyasooriya, Y. Ohbayashi, M. Hariyama and M. Kameyama, "Memory Allocation Exploiting Temporal Locality for Reducing Data-Transfer Bottlenecks in Heterogeneous Multicore Processors", IEEE Transactions on Circuits and Systems for Video Technology, Vol.21, No.10, pp.1453-1466, 2011.

[6] H. M. Waidyasooriya, M. Hariyama and M. Kameyama, "Architecture of an FPGA-Oriented Heterogeneous Multi-core Processor with SIMD-Accelerator Cores", International Conference on Engineering of Reconfigurable Systems and Algorithms (ERSA), pp.179-186, 2010.

[7] http://www.xilinx.com/products/boards-and-kits/ EK-Z7-ZC702-G.htm

[8] M. Hariyama, H. Sasaki, and M. Kameyama, "Architecture of a stereo matching VLSI processor based on hierarchically parallel memory access", IEICE Trans. Inform. Syst., Vol.E88-D, No.7, pp.1486.1491, 2005.

On-demand Fault Scrubbing Using Adaptive Modular Redundancy

Naveed Imran, Rizwan A. Ashraf, and Ronald F. DeMara
Department of Electrical Engineering and Computer Science
University of Central Florida, Orlando, FL 32816-2362, United States

Abstract— *We present an architectural framework for N-Modular Redundant (NMR) systems exploiting the dynamic partial reconfiguration capability of FPGAs. Partial reconfiguration is used to dynamically construct the throughput datapath under failure conditions. The throughput datapath utilizes only one instance of a Functional Element (FE) while the other instances undergo evaluation by being subjected to the same actual inputs to the system. A software-based process is shown to be sufficient to periodically monitor the health of the active and standby FEs, thus avoiding a hardware voter in the datapath. The defective behavior of an active FE triggers the reconfiguration process and consequently a healthy element is introduced into the datapath. Meanwhile, sustainability is increased by refurbishing faulty FEs using Genetic Algorithms (GAs) to circumvent aging or radiation-induced hard faults. Furthermore, the configuration bitstreams are protected in the flash memory using Reed-Solomon codes to provide multi-bit block correction. Together, this hybrid of adaptive modular redundancy and online error correction is shown to provide fault coverage at very low latency overhead.*

Keywords: SRAM-based FPGAs, Reconfiguration Techniques for Fault-handling, Evolvable Hardware, Autonomous Operation, Semiconductor Aging, Hard/Permanent Fault Refurbishment

1. Introduction

Intelligent self-healing capability is desirable in microelectronics based systems which can be achieved through biologically-inspired design paradigms. Adaptive designs seek to increase sustainability of circuit operation when subject to aging-induced degradation which is increasingly prominent with reduced feature size. The need to mitigate radiation effects experienced by SRAM-based FPGAs in space applications provides an additional motivation for exploring fault handling schemes. FPGAs are prone to faults in the logic resources as well in the configuration memory, such as Single Event Upsets (SEUs) [1]. *Scrubbing* is an established technique of in-situ fault-mitigation [1], [2]. Scrubbing consists of rewriting the configuration memory with a fault-free bitstream to eliminate any SEU occurrences which have corrupted the configuration logic.

Previous external scrubbing techniques rely on a fault-free "golden" copy of the bitstream to be available at all times. Traditionally, the reference bitstream resides in an external storage device [2] which is considered to be a golden element. We avoid this assumption of a failsafe storage device as even flash memories are susceptible to faults due to space radiation effects [3]. Thus to achieve sustainability, consideration of error correcting codes can be worthwhile to protect the bitstreams in a storage media.

The proposed *On-demand Fault Scrubbing* technique utilizes a Reed-Solomon error correcting decoder implemented using the on-chip PowerPC processor. In the prototype, the processor fetches a partial bitstream from the Compact Flash, decodes it, and writes the decoded bitstream to the configuration memory through the Xilinx *Internal Configuration Access Port* (ICAP) port. Adaptive modular redundancy utilizes dynamic reconfiguration to adjust redundancy during computation. The proposed system can operate in simplex mode where only one instance is active and the periodic scrubbing provides a basic level of fault tolerance. To further increase reliability, an FE is replicated thereby introducing redundancy into the design. The majority voting of the output of FEs is performed for fault detection, or to identify the health of these modules using NMR. To sustain a pool of healthy modules, faulty FEs are refurbished by a GA using mutation and crossover operations at the physical-resource level. Autonomous fault-handling capability is achieved in presence of faults, without needing manual intervention.

2. Related Work

The homogeneous nature of FPGA *Configuration Logic Blocks (CLBs)* allows development of generic testing schemes to detect faults in the logic resources. Emmert, Stroud, and Abramovici [4] proposed an online *Built-In Self-Test (BIST)* technique for mitigating hardware faults in FPGAs. For this purpose, *Roving Self-Test AReas (STARs)* are subjected to test pattern inputs and the output response of the contained resources is analyzed to detect faults. The *Cyclic NMR* technique [5] is based upon functional testing of resources, yet at a coarse granularity to improve fault isolation latency and fault recovery period. In contrast to *resource-based testing* schemes, *functional-based testing* schemes utilize the intrinsic functionality of a *Circuit Under Test (CUT)* without applying additional test inputs.

Evolutionary techniques for fault tolerance have been proposed in literature with the objective of either designing fault-insensitive circuits or achieving runtime refurbishment of faults. Keymeulen et al. [6] demonstrated the ability of GAs to realize fault-insensitive Field Programmable Analog

52

Int'l Conf. Reconfigurable Systems and Algorithms | ERSA'13 |

Array (FPAA) designs for increased survivability of electronics used in space missions. On the other hand, runtime refurbishment provides sustainable functionality when permanent faults occur due to unforeseen events such as aging.

Traditionally, Hamming codes have been applied in memory systems to correct single bit errors. Their implementation is straightforward, yet their fault-handling capacity in terms of the number of erroneous bits per block is low. On the other hand, more advance techniques like Reed-Solomon error correcting codes provide higher fault capacity, at the expense of increased logic complexity in the correction circuit. For flash memories in particular, various error correction schemes have been evaluated in the literature [7]. As the need for reconfiguration in SRAM-based FPGAs is much less frequent than that of accessing data in a SRAM memory storage device, the latency overhead of a sophisticated error scheme can be justified. Therefore, we investigate using Reed-Solomon codes to protect configuration bitstreams. In addition, the logic complexity of the error correcting scheme is of less concern since our software-based decoder runs on an embedded processor. Exposures to failures in the PowerPC have been addressed in recent work [8] using a radiation-hardened controller to monitor the health of the PowerPC within the FPGA fabric. Moreover, in the technique proposed herein, the PowerPC is not on the critical throughput path, so its catastrophic failure would impair only the recovery capability rather than the output correctness.

Previous methods for configuration memory protection employ scrubbing schemes. A basic scrubbing scheme performs readback of the configuration memory and if any error is found in a particular frame, then only the corresponding frame is overwritten [2]. On the other hand, NASA's *(Radiation Effects and Analysis Group)* proposed an external blind scrubbing method in which configuration memory is periodically overwritten by a golden bitstream. An internal scrubber utilizing a PicoBlaze processor softcore was proposed by Heiner et al. [9]. However, multiple bit upsets are challenging to accommodate when using *Single Error Correction, Double Error Detection* codes described therein. We exploited the high error correcting capability of Reed-Solomon codes to handle multiple bit errors in the configuration bitstream.

3. Adaptive Modular Redundancy with On-demand Scrubbing

The hardware architecture of our proposed approach is shown in the Fig. 1. An on-chip PowerPC processor monitors the throughput for any discrepancy while the other on-chip processor is employed to perform refurbishment. An NMR configuration consists of N instances of a given FE, where all of them are subjected to the same input. An *Active FE* is defined as the FE whose datapath is directly connected to the output of the system. The outputs from both the active and

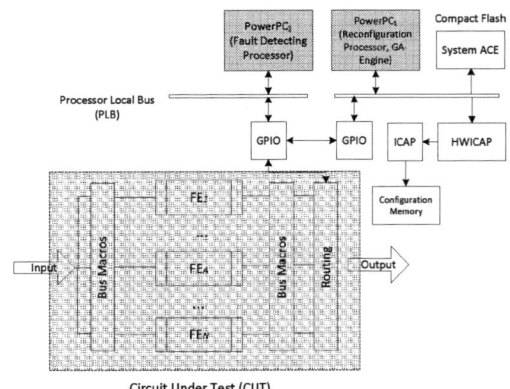

Fig. 1: Adaptive Redundancy based Hardware Architecture

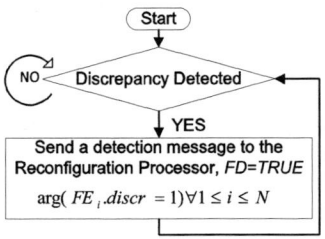

Fig. 2: Flowchart of Fault Detection Process

standby FEs are communicated through the GPIO and PLB to the PowerPC software which monitors the health of these elements. After an *Evaluation window*, E, the software based voter updates the health status of the FEs based upon their discrepant behavior. The functional resources in datapath as well as the resources under test are evaluated with the actual throughput data inputs to the system instead of any synthetic test vectors. Upon identification of a faulty PE, the GA-based refurbishment mechanism is initiated to circumvent faults in the mapped design.

Fig. 2 and Fig. 3 illustrate the flow of the fault-handling mechanism. Initially, multiple copies of a given FE are instantiated in various partial reconfigurable regions. The software-based discrepancy monitor implemented by *Fault Detecting Processor* periodically observes outputs to detect discrepancies between the output of individual FEs and the majority of their outputs. Intermittent sampling removes the hardware voter from the throughput path and is appropriate for applications such as signal processing in which checking of every output is not essential to maintain viable throughput. Any discrepant behavior detected by the PowerPC results in that FE to be marked as faulty. If the active FE in the datapath becomes faulty, the system's main output port is transferred to that of one of healthy FEs. In this way, a

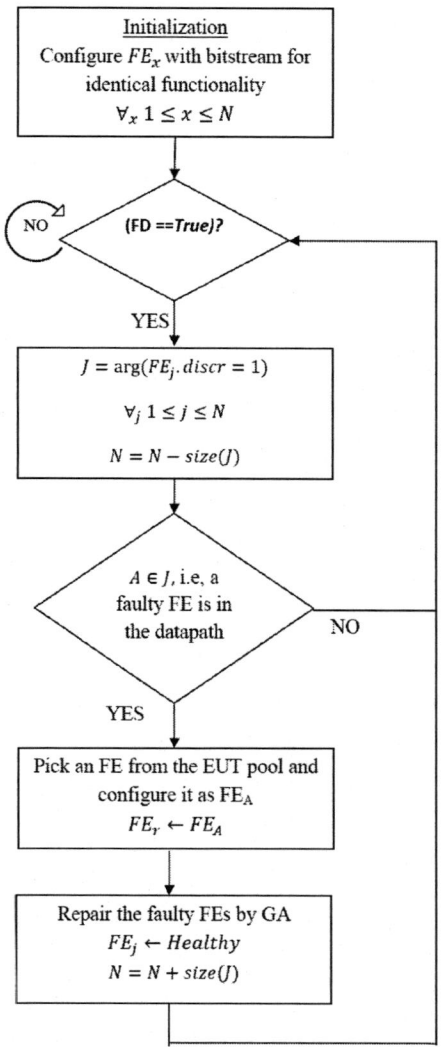

Fig. 3: Flowchart of Fault Recovery Process

Table 1: Reconfig. latency for improved correction capability

Codeword Length, n	Fault Capacity, t	Reconfiguration Time (msec), λ
15	3	609
17	4	774
19	5	976
21	6	1213

healthy FE is inserted in the datapath and becomes the new *Active FE* as illustrated in Fig. 3. Thus, the system is reconfigured with minimum latency to maintain system throughput. Meanwhile, the *Refurbishment Processor* on second PowerPC controls the reconfiguration mapping for fault recovery. As a proof-of-concept system, the GA is currently implemented on the host PC to refurbish faulty FEs outside the critical path so as to keep all N FEs healthy.

4. Experimental Setup and Results

For the proof of concept, MCNC benchmarks circuits [10] have been used to study the proposed dynamic NMR arrangement, bitstreams encoding, and GA-based refurbishment techniques. First, a 32-input with 32-output MCNC benchmark circuit C6288 is implemented on a Xilinx de-

velopment board ML410. This board has a Virtex-4 FPGA on it and the synthesized circuit occupies 752 LUTs (or 427 slices) for one instantiation. The PowerPC is instantiated by Xilinx Platform Studio. The project is managed in Xilinx ISE, and the partial bitstream files are generated using PlanAhead. The partial bitstreams for the FEs are stored in compact flash which is interfaced to the processor through the System ACE controller.

For NMR of size N=5, a total of 5 instances of a benchmark circuit are created at design time. Five partial reconfiguration regions are defined whose sizes depend upon the application circuits. The partial bitstream size of an FE is 38KBytes whereas that of a blank bistream is 11KByte. In their original approach, Reed and Solomon represented a message of length k by a polynomial $p(x)$. The coefficients of this polynomial are the source symbols. The polynomial $p(x)$ is over-sampled to provide some redundancy in the information and the resultant codeword is sent over the noisy channel. Thus, a Reed-Solomon encoder [11] is specified as $RS(n, k)$ where: k = number of data symbols with s-bit each in the original message, and n = number of symbols in the codeword after appending parity symbols. The receiver end recovers the original message by solving a linear system of equations. The error correction capability, t of a Reed-Solomon decoder is given by [11]: $t = \frac{(n-k)}{2}$. Thus, the decoder can correct up to t symbols in the codeword. In $RS(15,9)$, each codeword contains 15 symbols out of which 9 are data symbols and 6 are parity symbols. For evaluating the error correcting code scheme for memory protection, faults are randomly injected into the encoded bitstream stored on a compact flash. Bitstream errors reasonably mimic the effect of radiations on an FPGA device. The PowerPC's software based Reed-Solomon decoder extracts the actual bitstream from the encoded bitstream, and it is observed that these faults are correctable as far as the number of errors are less than half of the difference between the encoded message size and the data block size [11]. Although, the Reed-Solomon decoder has currently a software based implementation, it can be implemented in hardware in future work.

Table 1 lists reconfiguration time overhead when using the proposed fault tolerant architecture. In simplex mode, only one instance of an FE is instantiated whereas it is replicated 5 times in the NMR case. The size of the RS encoded partial bitstream increases from its original size, thereby increasing the reconfiguration time as listed which includes the time for decoding. For typically-sized circuits,

Table 2: GA Refurbishment Results for various sized circuits

	c17	cm42a	3-to-8 decoder	cm85a	3x3 Multiplier	misex1	Z9sym
No. of LUTs	8	20	24	36	40	72	148
Max. Fitness	64	160	64	6144	384	1792	512
Fault Impact	46	159	57	6120	327	1648	420
Avg. no of Generations	105	529	169	113.1	1428	77297	60195
95% Confidence Interval	102, 109	428,630	145,193	92.6,133.6	1018,1837	51129,103464	60195,60195
No. of Runs	20	20	20	20	20	20	1

the logic and memory resource overhead of NMR can be justifiable within the capacity of current multi-million gate-equivalent FPGAs and gigabyte capacity flash memories.

To study fault effects in logic resources, multiple *stuck-at* faults are injected in the post-place and route simulation model of the circuit. It is observed that the output deviates from the truth-table of the circuit. The *Evaluation Window* depends upon the circuit and the quality of throughput desired. The reconfiguration time of a faulty PE is not in the critical path and may be neglected when considering the total time for fault isolation and recovery.

Next, experiments were conducted to determine a tractable size of the circuit that the GA can refurbish in the presence of fault(s). Circuits with various extents of LUTs utilization were selected to assess GA-based refurbishment feasibility with increasing number of LUTs. The experiments were performed on a platform which models a FPGA circuit composed of 4-input LUTs. A custom synthesis cell library was built to map the benchmark circuits on to a predefined subset of LUT functions supported by the platform. The circuits were mapped using the ABC synthesis tool [12]. The software platform implements a conventional finite population GA. GA operators of mutation and crossover are supported with tournament-based selection and elitism to maintain best performing individuals over time.

The results of refurbishment experiments are demonstrated in Table 2 for the benchmark circuits of c17 (5 inputs, 2 outputs), cm42a (4, 10), 3-to-8 decoder, cm85a (11, 3), 3x3 multiplier, misex1 (8, 7) and Z9sym (9, 1) with population size of 50. The population size was decreased to 20 for experiments with the following benchmarks: cm85a, misex1 and Z9sym. The GA terminates upon achieving the preset fitness threshold, thus sufficiently refurbishing functionality to the specified level. The results indicate the effect on the performance of the GA while increasing the number of LUTs utilized and also increasing number of output lines.

5. Discussion

In the fault-handling technique developed herein, by continually keeping all the FEs in operation, the fault capacity of a system is improved to tolerate multiple failures. Upon fault-detection, a faulty module in the datapath is replaced by one of the healthy modules in the test pool. Meanwhile, the faulty module can be refurbished by using GAs without impeding the operational datapath. The scheme can be conceptualized as if only one FE is active, other resources periodically undergo test. However, the resources under test are evaluated to actual inputs at all times, which is also useful in verifying the health of the active FE. As opposed to resource-based testing schemes, this functional testing scheme maintains throughput for the inputs which are actually used rather than exhaustive testing of the resources by additional test vectors. The recovery results of experiments for various benchmark circuits demonstrate the effectiveness of the proposed scheme for adaptive runtime refurbishment.

References

[1] N. Rollins, M. Fuller, and M. Wirthlin, "A comparison of fault-tolerant memories in SRAM-based FPGAs," in *Aerospace Conference, 2010 IEEE*, pp. 1 –12, March 2010.

[2] M. Berg, C. Poivey, D. Petrick, D. Espinosa, A. Lesea, K. LaBel, M. Friendlich, H. Kim, and A. Phan, "Effectiveness of internal versus external seu scrubbing mitigation strategies in a Xilinx FPGA: Design, test, and analysis," *Nuclear Science, IEEE Transactions on*, vol. 55, pp. 2259 –2266, Aug. 2008.

[3] F. Irom and D. N. Nguyen, "Radiation tests of highly scaled high density commercial nonvolatile flash memories," tech. rep., Jet Propulsion Laboratory Pasadena, California, 2008.

[4] J. Emmert, C. Stroud, and M. Abramovici, "Online fault tolerance for FPGA logic blocks," *Very Large Scale Integration (VLSI) Systems, IEEE Transactions on*, vol. 15, pp. 216 –226, Feb. 2007.

[5] N. Imran and R. F. DeMara, "Cyclic NMR-based fault tolerance with bitstream scrubbing via Reed-Solomon codes," in *Presentations at the ReSpace/MAPLD Conference*, Aug. 2011.

[6] D. Keymeulen, A. Stoica, R. Zebulum, S. Katkoori, P. Fernando, H. Sankaran, M. Mojarradi, and T. Daud, "Self-reconfigurable analog array integrated circuit architecture for space applications," in *Adaptive Hardware and Systems, 2008. AHS '08. NASA/ESA Conference on*, pp. 83–90, 2008.

[7] B. Chen, X. Zhang, and Z. Wang, "Error correction for multi-level nand flash memory using reed-solomon codes," in *Signal Processing Systems, 2008. SiPS 2008. IEEE Workshop on*, pp. 94 –99, Oct. 2008.

[8] M. Bucciero, J. P. Walters, and M. French, "Software fault tolerance methodology and testing for the embedded PowerPC," in *Aerospace Conference, 2011 IEEE*, pp. 1–9.

[9] J. Heiner, N. Collins, and M. Wirthlin, "Fault tolerant ICAP controller for high-reliable internal scrubbing," in *Aerospace Conference, 2008 IEEE*, pp. 1 –10, March 2008.

[10] S. Yang, "Logic synthesis and optimization benchmarks version 3," tech. rep., Microelectronics Center of North Carolina, 1991.

[11] M. Riley and I. Richardson, "An introduction to Reed-Solomon codes: principles, architecture and implementation," 1996. Retrieved on Nov. 02, 2011 [Online] http://www.cs.cmu.edu/afs/cs/project/pscico-guyb/realworld/www/reedsolomon/reed_solomon_codes.html.

[12] Berkeley Logic Synthesis and Verification Group, "ABC: A system for sequential synthesis and verification," Retrieved on May 31, 2013 [Online] http://www.eecs.berkeley.edu/alanmi/abc/.

Reducing Floating-Point Error Based on Residue-Preservation and Its Evaluation on an FPGA

Hasitha Muthumala Waidyasooriya, Hirokazu Takahashi, Yasuhiro Takei,
Masanori Hariyama and Michitaka Kameyama
Graduate School of Information Sciences, Tohoku University
Aoba 6-6-05, Aramaki, Aoba, Sendai, Miyagi, 980-8579, Japan
Email: {hasitha, hirokazu, takei, hariyama, kameyama}@ecei.tohoku.ac.jp

Abstract—*Although scientific computing is gaining many attentions, calculations using computers always associated with arithmetic errors. Since computers have limited hardware resources, rounding is necessary. When using iterative computations, the rounding errors are added and propagated through the whole computation domain so that the final results can be completely wrong. In this paper, we propose a floating-point error reduction method and its hardware architecture for addition. The proposed method is based on preserving the residue coursed by rounding and reusing the preserved value in next iteration. The evaluation shows that the proposed method gives almost the same accuracy as the conventional double-precision floating point computation. Moreover, using the proposed method is 24% area efficient than using a conventional double-precision adder.*

Keywords: Precise arithmetic, floating-point, FPGA.

1. Introduction

Scientific computing is an area where mathematical models are executed in computers to analyze and simulate various physical behaviors. Such simulations are used in many fields such as fluid dynamics, molecular analysis and even in rocket science. Many of such models use repeated calculations spans many iterations. For example, finite-difference time-domain (FDTD) [1] used in fluid dynamics is such a well know method that deals with solving differential equations in a time-domain.

Although scientific computing is gaining many attentions due to the introduction of multicore CPUs and many core GPUs, calculations using computers are always associated with arithmetic errors. Due to the limited hardware resources in computers, rounding of the computation results is necessary. This gives a small error in many computations. Although such errors are negligible in a single calculation, they are a very big problem in scientific computing. The simulation models use repeated calculations with thousands of iterations to produce a result. Therefore, small error in each iteration add up and propagated through the whole computation domain. Due to this, the final results obtained after thousands of iterations might be completely wrong. Computation errors are been discussed in many works such

as [2] and [3]. Accepting those results could bring devastating effects since many simulations are connected with real world application such as air plane designing, power plant controlling etc.

Easiest way of reducing computation error is to add more precision [4]. However, that comes with an increased hardware cost. Using software libraries such as "multiple precision integers and rationals (MPIR)" [5] is another way of dealing with this problem. However, when the precision increases the processing time also increases exponentially. In this paper, we focus on floating-point addition and propose a error-reduction method and its area-efficient hardware implementation. The proposed method based on a very simple idea of preserving the residue due to rounding and reuse it in recursive computation. We propose an efficient method implement this algorithm in smaller number of time steps. According to the evaluation using FPGA, the proposed single-precision floating-point adder gives almost the same accuracy of the double-precision floating-point adder, but requires 24% less area compared to the conventional double-precision adder.

2. Floating-point error reduction using residue-preservation

In this section, we focus on reducing the floating-point error due to normalization and rounding in iterative computations. In these computations, the output of the iteration i is used as an input of iteration $i + 1$. Therefore, the error is propagated from iteration to iteration. However, if we can keep the residue of rounding in one iteration, we can use it in the next iteration. Even if the residue is very small during a single iteration, it will become large if we keep storing it. Therefore, after many iterations, the residue of rounding is also add up to the result and that will reduce the error. The algorithm to reduce the floating-point error in summation is given as follows.

Step 1: $R = S_0 = 0$
Step 2: $U = R + X_i$
Step 3: $S_{i+1} = S_i + U$
Step 4: $V = S_{i+1} - S_i$
Step 5: $R = U - V$

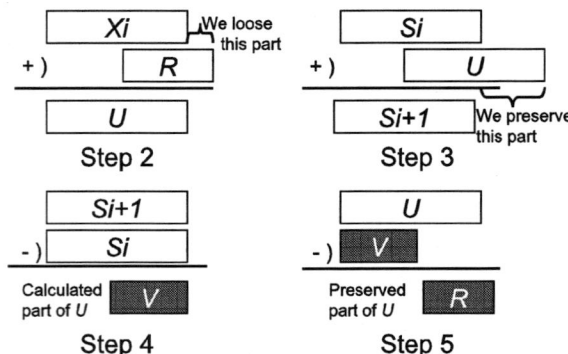

Fig. 1: Floating-point error reduction method

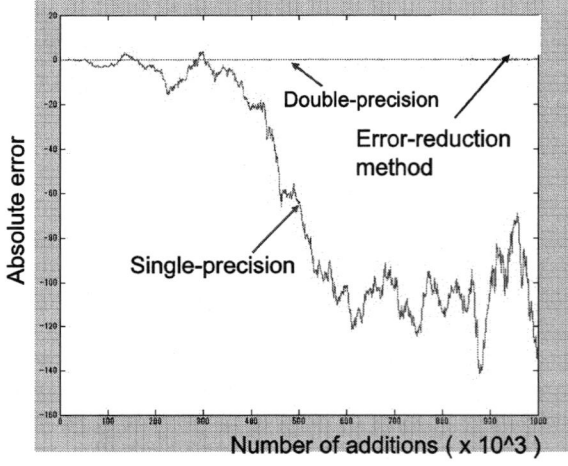

(a) Computation error vs. number of additions

Step 6: if($i < n$), increase i by 1 and go to Step 2
       else, finish

Figure 1 explains this algorithm using the computation of $\sum_{n=0}^{n-1} X_i$ as an example. In the first iteration, the value X_i is added with the residue R of the previous step. The result is saved as U as shown in Step 2. In this calculation, we loose a part of R due to rounding. Then we add U to the sum S_i to get the new summation S_{i+1}. Due to the rounding, only a part of U is added. This part V is found in Step 4. To find the non-added part of U, we subtract V from U in Step 4. Since this part is not added to the summation yet, we preserve it as R and use it in the next iteration.

Figure 2 shows the evaluation of this method. When the number of computations are large, this error reduction method with single precision computation gives extremely better results compared to conventional single-precision computation as shown in Fig.2(a). Moreover, the error reduction method gives very similar results to the conventional double precision computation. Note that, we calculate the error compared to the double-precision computation so that the error of doable-precision becomes zero. Figure 2(b) shows the graphs of the error reduction method and conventional double precision method to see the difference more clearly. There are two reasons for this difference. The first one is the rounding occurs in the conventional double precision computation. The second one is the unused residue occurs in the addition of X_i and R in Step 2 as shown in Fig.1.

Although this method gives a very good computation results, it has so many steps and need two additions and two subtractions. Therefore, if available, it is better to use a high-precision computation than using the error reduction method with low-precision computation. However, in the next section, we propose an improved algorithm combined with a new floating-point adder architecture to get the same error reduction under less additional computation and small hardware overhead.

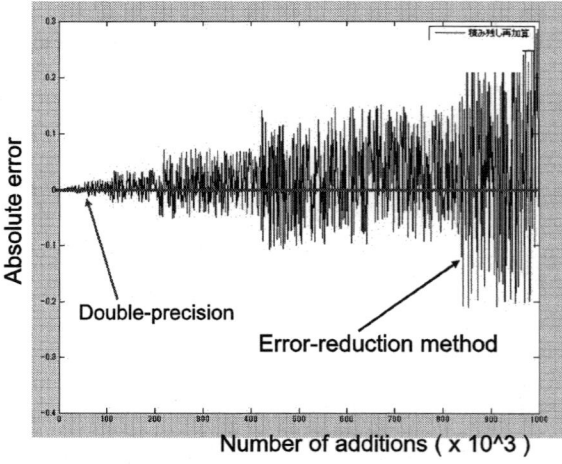

(b) Enlarged capture of Fig.2(a)

Fig. 2: Evaluation of the computation error

3. Proposed error reduction algorithm and its FPGA implementation

In the error-reduction algorithm explained in Section 2, the processing time is wasted in Steps 4 and 5 to calculate the residue occurs due to the rounding of S_{i+1}. However, if we can preserve all the bits of S_{i+1} before rounding, we can find the residue easily. This method is show as follows.

Step 1: $R = S_0 = 0$
Step 2: $U = R + X_i$
Step 3: $S_{i+1} = S_i + U$
       $R =$ residue of rounded S_{i+1}
Step 4: if($i < n$), increase i by 1 and go to Step 2
       else, finish

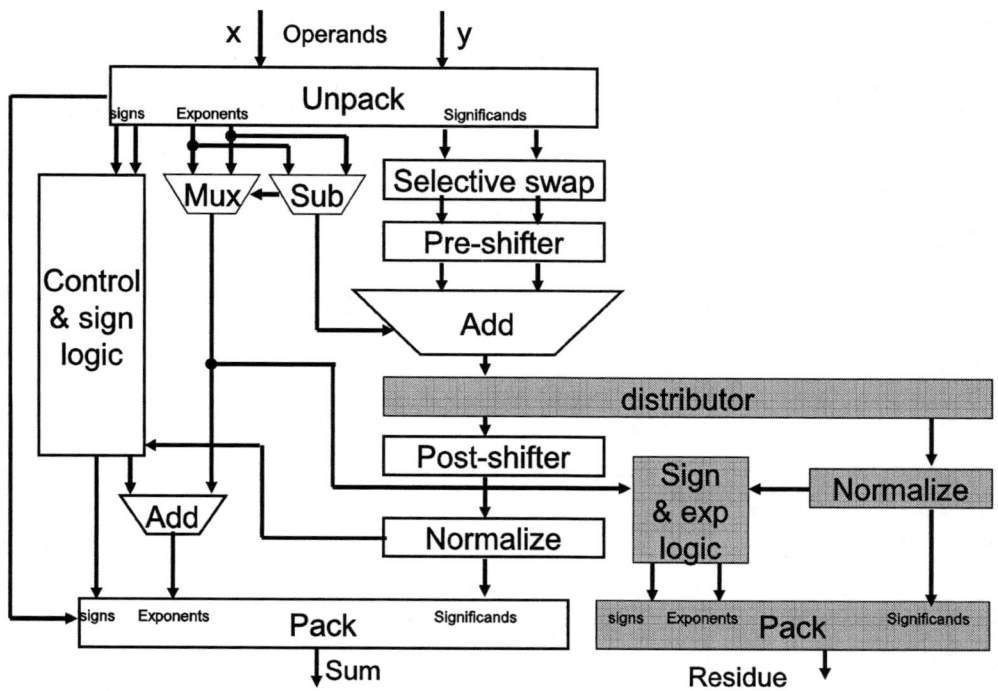

Fig. 3: Architecture of the proposed floating-point adder

Note that the residue calculation in Steps 4 and 5 are removed and the residue is preserved in Step 3.

To execute this algorithm, we proposes a new floating-point adder architecture as shown in Fig.3. The gray areas in Fig.3 shows the units we added to the conventional floating-point adder. To explain the architecture and the proposed algorithm, let us consider single-precision floating point addition. The "Add" unit shown in Fig,3 is the same one used in conventional single-precision adder. The only difference is that it produces two outputs; the normalized addition result and the residue after normalization and rounding. Since no extra adders are included, this architecture can be implemented area efficiently.

4. Evaluation

We implement the proposed floating-point adder on "Cyclone II EP2C35F6'2C6" FPGA to evaluate the error-reduction method. We used "Quartus II" software tool to calculate the number of logic elements (LEs) and the clock frequency. In the evaluation, the proposed method is compared with conventional single-precision and double-precision floating-point computations. Note that, we did not use any pipelines when implementing different adders. It is difficult to compare adders with different precisions with different pipeline stages.

Table 1 shows the evaluation results. According to the results, the proposed method requires less area than conven-

Table 1: FPGA evaluation of floating-point adders

	Conventional single-precision floating-point	Conventional double-precision floating-point	Proposed single-precision floating-point
Frequency	38 MHz	31 MHz	27 MHz
Num. LEs	611	1336	1014

tional double-precision floating-point method. However, the clock frequency is slightly lower than that of the double-precision method. As discussed in the previous section, the accuracy of the proposed method is much better than the single-precision and almost the same as the double-precision. Therefore, using the proposed method with single-precision is area-effective than using double-precision. However, as shown in 2(b), if the number of iterations are extremely large as few millions, the difference between the proposed method and conventional double-precision method gets larger.

5. Conclusion

We have proposed a floating-point error reduction method and its hardware architecture for addition. The proposed method based on preserving the residue coursed by rounding and reusing the preserved value for the calculation. The proposed adder store the residue in registers so that re-calculating of residue is not required. The evaluation shows that the proposed method gives almost the same accuracy as the double-precision floating point computation and more area efficient than the double precision adder. In future works, we will extend the proposed method of other computations such as multiplication and division.

Acknowledgment

This work is supported by MEXT KAKENHI Grant Number 12020735.

References

[1] H. S. Yee, "Numerical Solution of Initial Boundary Value Problems Involving Maxwell's Equations in Isotropic Media", IEEE Transactions on Antennas and Propagation, Vol.14, No.3, pp.302-307, 1966.

[2] B. Parhami, "Computer Arithmatic", Oxford University Press, 2010.

[3] M. Sofroniou and G. Spaletta, "Precise numerical computat", The Journal of Logic and Algebraic Programming, Vol.64, Issue 1, pp.113-134, 2005.

[4] Y. Hida , X. S. Li and D. H. Bailey, "Algorithms for Quad-Double Precision Floating Point Arithmetic", 15th IEEE Symposium on Computer Arithmetic, pp.155-162, 2001.

[5] http://www.mpir.org/

SESSION

BEST YOUNG ENTREPRENEUR; STUDENT RESEARCH CATEGORY

Chair(s)

Dr. Toomas Plaks
UK

ERSA-NVIDIA AWARD

"Best Young Entrepreneur"

Student Research Category

A Novel Parallel Computing Approach for Motion Estimation Based on Particle Swarm Optimization

Manal K. Jalloul

ECE Department, American University of Beirut, Beirut, Lebanon

Abstract *–Eventhough the area of video compression has existed for many decades, programming a coding algorithm is still a challenging problem. The actual bottleneck is to provide compressed video in real-time to communication systems. All those constraints have to be solved while keeping a good tradeoff between visual quality and compression rates. In this context, Motion Estimation (ME) is known to be a key operation. On the other hand, in the hardware industry, there is great emphasis on High Performance Computing (HPC) which is characterized by a shift to multi and many core systems. The programming community has to embrace the new parallelismin order to take advantage of the performance gains offered by the new technology. In this research work, we introduce a novel ME scheme with high level of data parallelism. It is capable of performing motion search for all the blocks of the frame in parallel using a modified Particle Swarm Optimization (PSO). This scheme can be implemented on Nvidia's massively parallel Graphical Processing Units (GPUs) to yield tremendous speedup as compared to existing techniques.*

Keywords: Motion Estimation, Parallel Computing, PSO, GPU, Multicore

1 Introduction

Today, video coding has become the central technology in a wide range of applications, as shown in Fig. 1. Some of these include digital TV, DVD, Internet streaming video, video conferencing, distance learning, surveillance, and security.

Video coding standards have evolved primarily through the development of the well-known ITU-T and ISO/IEC standards. The ITU-T produced H.261 and H.263, ISO/IEC produced MPEG-1 and MPEG-4 Visual, and the two organizations jointly produced the H.262/MPEG-2 Video and H.264/MPEG-4 AVC standards. Recently, these two organizations have been working together in a partnership known as the Joint Collaborative Team on Video Coding (JCT-VC) to produce the HEVC, the High Efficiency Video Coding standard, which is the most recent video coding standard. The first edition of the HEVC standard was finalized in January 2013[1].

Inter-prediction motion estimation is a common tool used in all video coding standards. The current H.264/MPEG-4 AVC video coding standard and the upcoming HEVCstandard employ the same hybrid approach to achieve high compression performance. Inter-prediction motion estimation is considered the most computationally intensive feature of the coding process.

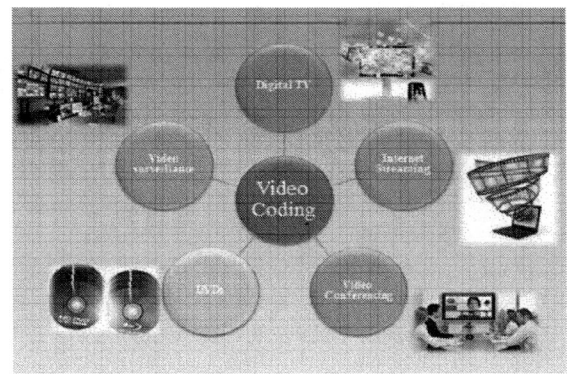

Figure 1Some applications of video coding

Efficient algorithms are needed to target the real-time processing requirements of emerging applications. Many fast search motion estimation algorithms have been developed to reduce the computational cost required by full-search algorithms. Fast search motion estimation techniques however often converge to a local minimum, which makes them subject to noise and matching errors.In this research work, we propose a novel fast and accurate block motion estimation algorithm based on an improved parallel PSO algorithm. The proposed scheme alleviates the problem of being trapped in local minima by employing the strategies of PSO. As a result, the proposed scheme produces a quality that outperforms most of the well-known fast searching techniques.

Today, we witness a high revolution in the hardware industry. There is a transition to multi-core and many-core systems which require a change in the programming approach to develop algorithms with high parallelism in order to take advantage of the high speedup provided by the available hardware. Existing ME algorithms are serial. They operate on blocks of the frame serially following the raster order. The proposed algorithm, on the other hand, exhibits high level of data parallelism. It performs motion estimation for all blocks of the frame in parallel. As a result, the proposed algorithm provides tremendous speedup and improved quality as compared to the exhaustive-search algorithm and to the well-known fast searching techniques.The proposed scheme will be implemented on the multi-core CPU architecture and the massively parallel architecture of the GPU using the NVIDIA CUDA platform and evaluated.

2   Technical description

Block-Matching Motion Estimation (BMME) with Full Search (FS) algorithm is the main computational burden in the video encoding process due to exhaustively search all possible blocks within the search window. Although FS algorithm can obtain the optimum motion vector (MV) in most cases, it consumes 60 to 80% of the total computational complexity. Thus, a fast and efficient motion estimation algorithm is required. In this research, we propose a novel fast and accurate block motion estimation algorithm based on an improved parallel Particle Swarm Optimization (PSO) algorithm.Since the proposed scheme is highly parallel, the massively parallel architecture of the GPU can be exploited to achieve massive speedup.

2.1   Related work

In the literature, two major approaches were researched to reduce the computational cost of the Exhaustive FS method. One employs fast mode decision algorithms to skip unnecessary block modes in variable block checking process [2-4]. The other one utilizes Fast Motion Estimation (FME) searching algorithms to reduce unnecessary search points.In the past years, the FME algorithms included three-step search [5], four-step search (4SS) [6] which can be generalized to N-step search (NSS), the diamond search (DS) methods [7], the cross-diamond search (CDS) method [8], and the Hexagon-based search [9]. In each of these fast search methods, a different search pattern is employed to reduce the number of search points. These algorithms reduce the computational complexity with negligible loss of image quality only when the motions matched the pattern well; otherwise, the image quality will decrease. In [10], a hybrid Unsymmetrical Multi-

Hexagon-grid search (UMHexagonS) algorithm, which attempt to usemany search patterns, has achieved both fast speed and good performance. In [11],Predictive Intensive Direction Searching (PIDS) algorithm was developed. PIDS successfully speeds up the process compared to UMHexagonS. However, this algorithm still searches each direction exhaustively, which may cause searching resource waste. In [12], a novel Predictive Priority Region Search (PPRS) algorithm that performs adaptively search indirection and locality regions was proposed. Other FME algorithms proposed in the literature include Motion adaptive search (MAS) [13], Variable Step Search (VSS) algorithm [14], and the Multi-Path Search (MPS) algorithm [15]. In addition to the above, several high efficiency algorithms were presented in the literature for ME that significantly reduce the number of checking points examined while retaining the video quality. These algorithms include the *Motion Vector Field Adaptive Search Technique* (MVFAST)[16], the *Predictive Motion Vector Field Adaptive Search Technique*(PMVFAST) [17], the *Advanced Predictive Diamond Zonal Search* (APDZS) [18], and the *Enhanced Predictive Zonal Search* (EPZS) [19].

Block matching motion estimation can be formulated into an optimization problem where one searches for the optimal matching block within a search region which minimizes RD cost. The above fast block matching methods suffer from poor accuracy since they dictate that only a very small fraction of the entire set of candidate blocks be examined, thereby making the search susceptible to beingtrapped into local optima on the error surface.In order to escape from the problem of local minima; several approaches were recently presented in the literature to use modern optimization algorithms to solve the problem of motion estimation. In [20, 22], the Genetic Algorithm (GA) has been considered for motion estimation. The proposed algorithms, however, tend to be complex and suffer from a high computational burden. In [22], the Simulated Annealing (SA) concept is employed to control searching process and to adaptively choose the intensive search region. In addition to GA and SA, there have been some attempts in the literature to apply Particle Swarm Optimization (PSO) to solve the problem of ME [23-29]. The PSO-based motion estimation methods introduced in [23-27] either have higher computational complexity [23] or have lower estimation accuracy [24, 25, 26] than several existing fast search methods.These algorithms try to improve the speed of convergence of the PSO iterations by choosing, as initial positions of the particles, the MVs of adjacent blocks in the frame as well as the (0,0) MV. The PSO iterations, however, can achieve faster convergence if we exploit the temporal correlation with the collocated block in the adjacent frame as well. In [29], a new variant of parallel particle swarm optimization (PPSO) known as small population-based modified PPSO (SPMPPSO) is proposed for fast motion estimation. In the standard PSO, positions of particles are updated after each individual fitness evaluation (i.e. in an asynchronous fashion or serially). The proposed algorithm in [29] achieves parallelism at the particle level, where the particles of the swarm evaluate the fitness function concurrently. Nevertheless, the algorithm presented in [29], as well as all the other PSO-based ME algorithms in the literature, operate serially on the blocks of a given frame following the raster order. Thus, if we can device a ME algorithm which can operate in parallel on all blocks of the frame, then the speed of the ME process could be tremendously enhanced. This is the main focus of our proposed PSO-based ME scheme.

2.2   Proposed approach

In this research work, we propose a new block matching algorithm based on a novel parallel PSO approach. The proposed algorithm allows performing motion estimation for all the macroblocks within the frame in parallel. To do that, a modified PSO algorithm is applied to all macroblocks concurrently for a certain number of iterations. After that, a synchronization step is performed among neighboring MBs to exchange information about the MVs found so far in the PSO process. Based on the assumption that the motion field is smooth and varies slowly, there are strong correlations between motion vectors of the neighboring blocks. As a result, this synchronization step allows making use of the spatial correlation characteristic between neighboring MBs to refine the MVs found so far in the PSO process. The proposed scheme exhibits intrinsic data parallelism and thus can be implemented on the CPU muti-core architecture and NVIDIA's GPU architecture using the CUDA platform to achieve the required speedup. To illustrate the proposed scheme, we first review the standard PSO algorithm, then we explain the details of our PSO-based parallel ME algorithm and compare it with the available schemes highlighting its estimated improvements.

2.2.1   The standard PSO algorithm

The PSO technique was introduced in [30] as a robust stochastic optimization technique based on a social-psychological model of social influence and social learning. Belonging to the category of swarm intelligence methods, PSO is a population-based technique inspired by the social behavior and movement dynamics of flocks of birds, schools of fish, and herds of animals adapting to their environment. In the conventional PSO approach, the so-called swarm is composed of a set of particles that are placed in a search space where each particle represents a candidate solution to a certain problem or function. Initially, each particle is assigned a randomized velocity. The particles then "fly" through a multidimensional search space, where the position of each particle is adjusted according to its own experience and that of its neighbors. Each particle keeps track of its personal best location (p_{best}) in the problem space, which represents the best solution (fitness) it has achieved so far. The location of the overall best value, obtained so far by any particle in the population, is called g_{best}. The PSO algorithm updates the position of a particle by moving the particle based on its past personal best (p_{best}) and the global best position (g_{best}) that has

been found by all the particles in the swarm. Details of the PSO iterations are shown in Fig. 2.

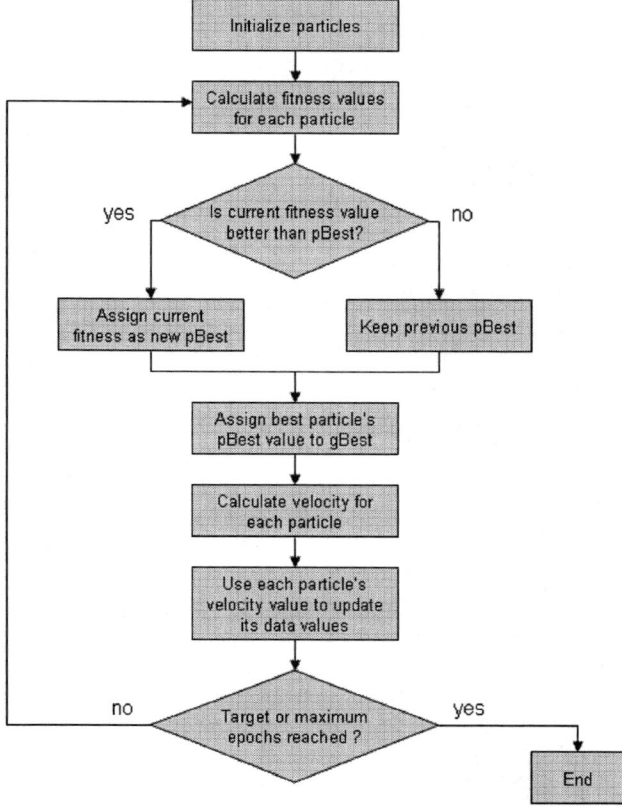

Figure 2 Iterations of the PSO algorithm.

The idea of PSO is to change the velocity of each particle towards its p_{best} and g_{best} locations at each time step. Acceleration is weighed by a random term, with separate random numbers being generated for acceleration toward the p_{best} and g_{best} locations. The velocity and position of a particle can be updated according to the following equations:

$$V_i(t+1) = wV_i(t) + c_1 r_1 [P_i(t) - X_i(t)] + c_2 r_2 [P_g(t) - X_i(t)] \quad (1)$$

$$X_i(t+1) = X_i(t) + V_i(t+1) \quad (2)$$

where i is the index of the particle, i = 1,2, . . . ,M; w the inertia weight; c_1, c_2 the positive acceleration constants; r_1, r_2 the random numbers, uniformly distributed within the interval [0, 1]; t the number of iterations so far; g the index of the best positioned particle among the entire swarm; P_i the position of p_{best} for the particle i; and P_g is the position of g_{best} for the entire swarm.

2.2.2   The proposed parallel PSO-based ME scheme

In this research work, we device a ME scheme which applies PSO strategies to find the optimal MVs for all the macroblocks of a given frame in parallel. This is done by executing the steps shown in Fig. 3.

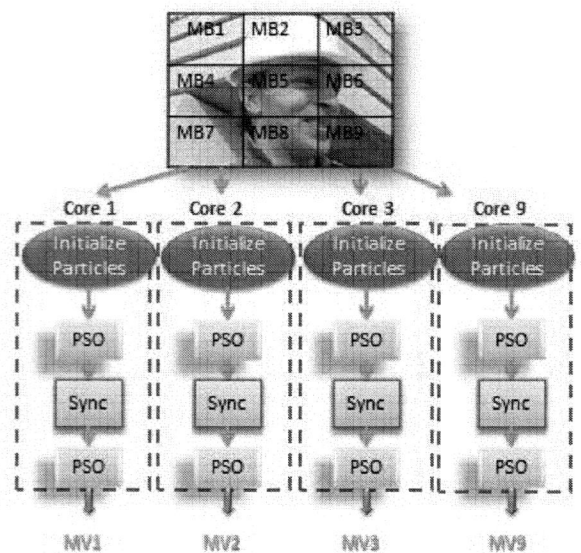

Figure 3Proposed motion estimation scheme

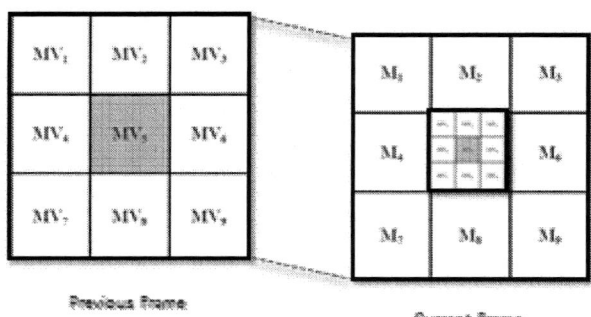

Figure 4Particlesinitialization of agiven MB

A given frame is divided into 16x16 macroblocks. Then, a swarm consisting of M particles is generated for each MB. Each particle of a given MB represents a matching MB within the search window in the reference frame. Using the PSO iterations, the positions of the particles is continuously updated until the global minimum of the Sum of Absolute Difference (SAD) cost function is reached.

In the standard PSO algorithm, the initial population is randomly selected, which brings high computational complexity to the motion search since the iterations are starting from random points which might be far from the global minimum. However, if the initial points are chosen to be close to the optimum, then faster convergence can be achieved. Since motion vectors have a high temporal correlation feature, we initialize 9 particles of each MB to the MVs of the collocated MB in the previous frame as well as its 8 adjacent neighbors. We also initialize one of the particles to the (0, 0) MV to account for static blocks. The rest of the M particles are randomly generated. Notice that at this point, we cannot use the MVs of the adjacent blocks in the same frame since these MVs are not calculated yet and the only apriori information we have is the motion of the MBs of the previous frame. This initialization step is shown in Fig. 4.

After initialization, the swarms of particles of all MBs are allowed to run for a predefined K number of iterations in parallel. During each iteration, each MB with index j adjusts the positions and velocities of its particles, independently from other MBs, evaluates the fitness function at the new positions, then it updates the values of P_{ij} and P_{gj} which are the position of the best fitness attained so far for particle i and the global best position for MB_j respectively. Early termination of search is allowed here whenever the fitness value is less than a predefined threshold value T_{th}.

After the K iterations are completed by all MBs of the frame, a synchronization step is performed to refine the MVs found so far in the PSO process. This is done by exploiting the high spatial correlation existing between MVs of neighboring blocks. To do that, each MB_j sorts its M particles in a decreasing order according to their P_{ij} values. Then the last 8 particles which have the worst P_{ij} values are eliminated and replaced by 8 new particles which are initialized to the P_g values of its 8 neighboring MBs.

In this synchronization step, neighboring MBs are allowed to refine their motion search process using information from neighboring blocks. Weak particles having the worst fitness values are replaced with strong particles which are located closer to the global optimum. This process is expected to speed up the convergence of the PSO algorithm. Communication between neighboring MBs is required in this step where each MB will broadcast to its 8 neighbors the value of it global best location P_g found so far in the motion search process. This process is shown in Fig. 5.

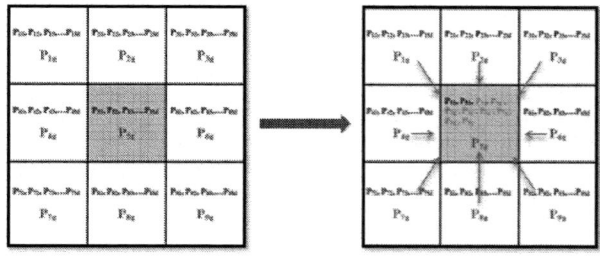

Figure 5 MB synchronization

2.3 Preliminary results

2.3.1 Estimation Accuracy

In order to test the accuracy of the proposed scheme, simulations were carried out on video sequences of various motion content in the QCIF format at 30 frames per second.The searching range is ±7 pixels and the block size is 16x16 pixels. The other parameters of simulation are as follows. For PSO, the size of the particle population was chosen to be M=10, N_{max}=12, N_{same}=4, K=6 so that only one synchronization point is needed, c_1 and c_2 are equal to 2.05.

Int'l Conf. Reconfigurable Systems and Algorithms | ERSA'13 |

65

The results interms of Peak Signal to Noise Ratio (PSNR) are given in table 1.

As shown in Fig.6, our proposed PSO algorithm performs very close to FS algorithm and exceeds that of all other schemes. Consequently, the proposed PSO algorithm has very high search accuracy.

Table 1Comparison of average PSNR results in db

Sequence	FS	DS	TSS	4SS	ARPS	PSO [14]	PSO new
Foreman	33.52	33.29	33.24	33.28	33.19	33.12	33.44
Bus	24.21	23.52	23.45	23.46	23.26	23.91	24.19
News	28.19	21.38	22.69	21.51	26.29	27.99	28.10
Stefan	25.14	24.53	24.97	24.56	24.92	25.03	25.11
Soccer	22.97	21.93	22.14	21.93	22.02	22.18	22.77
Silent	35.69	35.43	35.55	35.41	35.30	35.39	35.56
Carphone	27.46	25.42	27.01	25.23	27.13	27.20	27.39

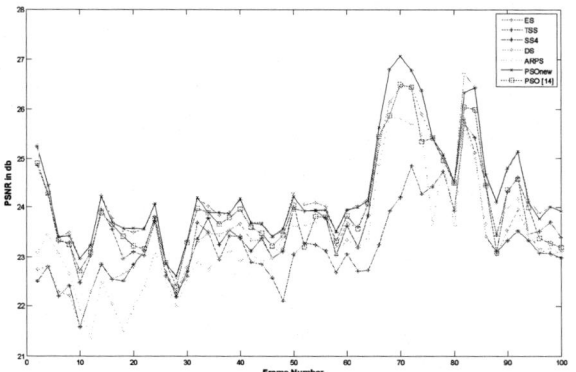

Figure 6 Motion estimation accuracyinterms of PSNR for Bus sequence

2.3.2 Speedup on multi-core processors

The proposed scheme exhibits a high level of data parallelism since it operates on all the blocks of the frame in parallel rather than serially as in existing ME approaches. As a result, our algorithm can be efficiently implemented on a multicore system. Therefore, a multicore implementation of our proposed algorithm is performed using the MATLAB® Parallel Computing Toolbox™ (PCT). The PCT provides parallel constructs in the MATLAB language, such as parallel for loops, distributed arrays and message passing & enables rapid prototyping of parallel code through an interactive parallel MATLAB session.

The proposed algorithm is simulated on a server with two Intel Xeon 2.66GHz CPU quad cores and 2GB memory. Thus, this server is equipped with 8 CPU cores. The execution platform is Matlab R2012a. Simulation results are given for Foreman sequence in QCIF format. The block size is 16x16 pixels. Thus, one frame of the QCIF (144x176) video sequence contains 9x11 blocks which should be mapped to the available cores to be processed in parallel.

Since the number of MBs in the frame is odd, we used an odd number of Matlab workers to perform simulations. For three available Matlab workers, each worker performs motion estimation for three rows of MBs in the frame. Whereas if nine Matlab workers are available, then each one performs motion estimation for one row of MBs within the frame. In this way, load balancing between the cores is ensured. The speedup obtained for 3 and 9 Matlab workers is given in table 2.

Table 2Speedup on multi-core CPU architecture

3 Matlab Workers	9 Matlab Workers
2.65	5.8

We notice that the speedup is high for three workers but not as high as expected for 9 workers. The reason behind this is that the available architecture contains only 8 cores. Although PCT allows to use upto 2 Matlab workers or labs per CPU core, but the performance will not be optimized.For a more thorough performance evaluation, simulations on a computer cluster with higher number of cores are still in progress.

2.3.3 Speedup on many-core GPU architecture

Nvidia GPUs are equipped with hundreds of decoupled cores that are capable of executing code in parallel. Our proposed scheme is in the process of being implemented on the GPU using the CUDA platform. Tremendous speedup is expected.

3 Impact and significance of the project

The significance of this research project lies in many folds. First, the topic under investigation is of great importance to the image and video processing industry. Motion estimation lies in the heart of any video compression system. It is the main block responsible for removing the temporal redundancies in a video sequence which allows achieving bit rate reduction and thus efficient compression. Developing an effective algorithm would improve the efficiency of the video codec to meet the needs of the evolving video industry. Cutting-edge applications such as HD video streaming, gaming, and mobile HDTV require high quality video at a very low bit-rate. Paving the way for next decade's video applications requires a video compression system with an optimized motion estimator.

Second, the method of investigation of this project tackles a novel approach that combines several important concepts. The proposed algorithm achieves parallelism which is the main requirement of all current algorithms to be able to use the state-of-the-art parallel processing capabilities to achieve speedup. In both industry and research today, there is a relentless pursuit of ever greater level of performance by employing parallelism. The advent of multicore CPUs and many-core GPUs means that mainstream processor chips are now parallel systems. Therefore, the challenge is to develop algorithms with intrinsic parallelism in order to exploit the capabilities of today's processors. So far, proposed Motion Estimation (ME) algorithms were either serial or had only partial parallelism. The algorithm presented in this proposal exhibits high data parallelism and thus can exploit the advance in the hardware industry. The proposed algorithm is to be implemented on the NVIDIA GPU architecture using the CUDA platform. The NVIDIA programmable GPU has evolved into a highly parallel, multithreaded, many-coreprocessor with tremendous computational horsepower and very high memory bandwidth [31]. Thus, an efficient and optimized implementation of our proposed ME algorithm on the GPU is expected to yield a tremendous amount of speedup.

On the other hand, the proposed algorithm is based on modern optimization which is now gaining much popularity in the academic and research field and is being used to solve problems in many fields.

Moreover, pursuing this research project would pave the way to many other projects in the future. A deep understanding of the problem and developing an effective algorithm would allow for exploring more improvements not only to the problem of motion estimation but to the other blocks of the video codec as well.

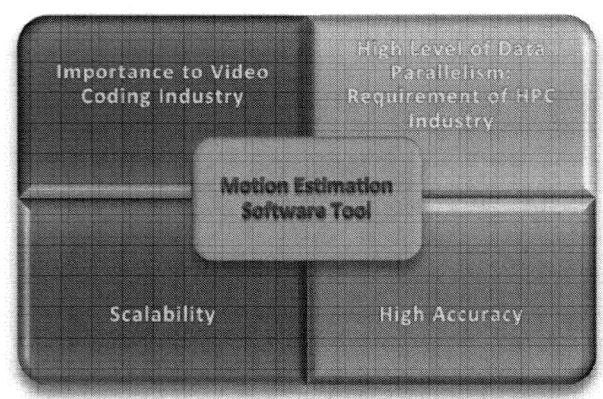

Figure 7Significance of the project

4 Conclusions

In this research project, we propose an efficient motion estimation software tool that is characterized by a high accuracy to meet the needs of the video coding industry. The proposed scheme also has a high level of data parallelism and thus can leverage the capabilities of today's High Performance Computing (HPC) industry to achieve speedup. Simulation results show that the proposed motion estimation tool yields better estimation accuracy than existing fast schemes. Preliminary implementation on a multi-core CPU architecture shows a high prospect of speedup obtained from available parallelism.

5 Acknowledgment

This research was supported by AUB's University Research Board. This work is part of my PhD thesis, so I would like to thank my advisor, Prof. Mohamad Adnan Al-Alaoui, and my PhD committee members for their guidance and positive feedback.

6 References

[1] G. J. Sullivan, J. R. Ohm, W. J. Han, T. Wiegand. "Overview of the High Efficiency Video Coding (HEVC) Standard" ; Circuits and Systems for Video Technology, IEEE Transactions on, Vol. No. 22, Issue No.12, pp.1649-1668, Dec. 2012.

[2] Jianfeng R., Kehtarnavaz N, and Budagavi M. "Computationally Efficient Mode Selection in H.264/AVC Video Coding" ; IEEE Trans. Consumer Electronics, vol. 54, pp. 877-886, 2008.

[3] Knesebeck M, Nasiopoulos P. "An Efficient Early-Termination Mode Decision Algorithm for H.264" ; IEEE Trans. Consumer Electronics, Vol. 55: pp. 1501-1510, 2009.

[4] D. Han, A. Kulkarni and K.R.Rao. "Fast Inter-prediction Mode Decision Algorithm for H.264 Video Encoder" ; 9th International Conference on Electrical Engineering/Electronics, Computer, Telecommunications and Information Technology (ECTI-CON), 16-18 May 2012.

[5] R. Li, B. Zeng, M.L. Liou. "A new three step search algorithm for block motion estimation"; IEEE Trans. Circuits Syst. Video Technol., Vol.4, Issue No.4, pp. 438–442, 1994

[6] L.M. Po, W.C. Ma. "A novel four-step search algorithm for fast block motion estimation" ; IEEE Trans. Circuits Syst. Video Technol., vol.6, no.3, pp. 313–317, 1996.

[7] S. Zhu, K. K. Ma. "A new diamond search algorithm for fast block-matching motion estimation" ; IEEE Transactions on Image Processing, vol. 9, pp. 287–290, 2000

[8] C. H. Cheung, L. M. Po. "A novel cross-diamond search algorithm for fast block motion estimation" ; IEEE Transactions on Circuits and Systems for Video Technology 12 (12) (2002) 1168–1177.

[9] C. Zhu, X. Lin, and L. P. Chau. "Hexagon-based search pattern for fast block motion estimation" ; IEEE Trans. Circuits Syst. Video Technol., vol. 12, no. 5, pp. 349–355, May 2002.

[10] Z. B. Chen, P. Zhou, and Y. He. "Fast Integer Pel and Fractional Pel Motion Estimation for JVT" ; in Proc. 6th Meeting: JVT–F017, Awaji Island, Japan, 2002.

[11] ZhiruShi, Fernando, W.A.C., De Silva, D.V.S.X. "A motion estimation algorithm based on Predictive Intensive Direction Search for H.264/AVC" ; IEEE Int. Conf. Multimedia and Expo (ICME), pp.667-672, July 2010.

[12] Zhiru Shi, W.A.C. Fernando and A. Kondoz. "An Efficient Fast Motion Estimation in H.264/AVC by Exploiting Motion Correlation Character" ; IEEE International Conference on Computer Science and Automation Engineering (CSAE), Vol. 3, pp. 298 – 302, 25-27 May 2012.

[13] P. I. Hosur. "Motion Adaptive Search for Fast Motion Estimation"; IEEE Trans. Consumer Electronics, vol. 49, pp. 1330-1340, 2003.

[14] KiBeom K, Young J, Min-Cheol H. "Variable Step Search Fast Motion Estimation for H.264/AVC Video Coder" ; IEEE Trans. Consumer Electronics, vol. 54: pp. 1281-1286, 2008.

[15] Goel S and Bayoumi M. A. "Multi-Path Search Algorithm for Block-Based Motion Estimation"; IEEE Int. Conf Image Processing, pp. 2373-2376, 2006.

[16] P.I. Hosur and K.K. Ma. "Motion Vector Field Adaptive Fast Motion Estimation"; Second International Conference on Information, Communications and Signal Processing (ICICS '99), Singapore, 7-10 Dec. 1999.

[17] A.M. Tourapis, O.C. Au, and M.L. Liou. "Predictive Motion Vector Field Adaptive Search Technique (PMVFAST) - Enhancing Block Based Motion Estimation" ; in proceedings of Visual Communications and Image Processing (VCIP-2001), pp.883-892, San Jose, CA, January 2001.

[18] A.M. Tourapis, O.C. Au, and M.L. Liou. "New Results on Zonal Based Motion Estimation Algorithms – Advanced Predictive Diamond Zonal Search" ; in proceedings of 2001 IEEE International Symposium on Circuits and Systems (ISCAS-2001), Vol. No. 5, pp.183–186, Sydney, Australia, May 6-9, 2001.

[19] A. M. Tourapis. "Enhanced predictive zonal search for single and multiple frame motion estimation" ;Electronic Imaging 2002.International Society for Optics and Photonics, pp. 1069-1079, 2002

[20] L.T. Hoand J.M. Kim. "Direction Integrated Genetic Algorithm for Motion Estimation in H.264/AVC" ;Advanced Intelligent Computing Theories and Applications. With Aspects of Artificial Intelligence Lecture Notes in Computer Science,Vol. No. 6216, pp. 279-286, 2010.

[21] A. El Ouaazizi, M. Zaim, & R. Benslimane. "A Genetic Algorithm for Motion Estimation" ; IJCSNS International Journal of Computer Science and Network Security, VOL.11 No.4, April 2011.

[22] Z. Shi, W.A.C. Fernando, and A. Kondoz. "Simulated Annealing for Fast Motion Estimation Algorithm in H.264/AVC" ; Simulated Annealing - Single and Multiple Objective Problems, Marcos de Sales Guerra Tsuzuki (Ed.), ISBN: 978-953-51-0767-5, InTech, DOI: 10.5772/50974. Available from: http://www.intechopen.com/books/simulated-annealing-single-and-multiple-objective-problems/simulated-annealing-for-fast-motion-estimation-algorithm-in-h-264-avc

[23] G.-Y. Du, T. S. Huang, L. X. Song, and B. J. Zhao." A novel fast motion estimation method based on particle swarm optimization";Fourth International Conference on Machine Learning and Cybernetics, 2005.

[24] K.M. Bakwad, S.S. Pattnaik, B.S. Sohi, S. Devi, S. Gollapudi, C.V. Sagar, and P.K. Patra. "Small population based modified parallel particle swarm optimization for motion estimation" ; 16th International Conference on Advanced Computing and Communications (ADCOM'2008), 2008.

[25] R. Ren, M.M. Manokar, Y. Shi, B. Zheng. "A Fast Block Matching Algorithm for Video Motion Estimation Based on Particle Swarm Optimization and Motion Prejudgement" ; 2006.

[26] X. Yuan, X. Shen." Block matching algorithm based on particle swarm optimization for motion estimation" ; International Conference on Embedded Software and Systems (ICESS'2008), 2008.

[27] Zhang Ping, Chen Hu, Wei Ping."Fast Motion Estimation Algorithm for Scalable Motion Coding" ; 2010 International Conference on Electrical and Control Engineering (ICECE), pp. 25-27, June 2010.

[28] Bakwad, Kamalakar M., Pattnaik, Shyam S., Sohi, B. S., Devi, Swapna, Gollapudi, Sastry V. R. S., Sagar, Ch. Vidya and Patra, P. K. "Fast Motion Estimation using Small Population-Based Modified Parallel Particle Swarm Optimisation" ; IJPEDS 26, no. 6, pp. 457-476, 2011.

[29] J. Cai, W. David Pan. "On Fast And Accurate Block-Based Motion Estimation Algorithms Using Particle Swarm Optimization" ; Information Sciences, Vol. No. 197, pp. 53–64, 15 August 2012.

[30] R. Poli, J. Kennedy, and T. Blackwell."Particle swarm optimization: an overview"; Swarm Intelligence 1, pp. 33–57, 2007.

[31] "NVIDIA CUDA Compute Unified Device Architecture, Programming Guide version 2.0", 2008, found on www.nvidia.com.

SESSION

INVITED LECTURE

Chair(s)

Dr. Toomas Plaks
UK

ERSA – INVITED TALK/LECTURE

Addressing the Challenges of Hardware Assurance in Reconfigurable Systems

William H. Robinson, Trey Reece, and Nihaar N. Mahatme
Security and Fault Tolerance (SAF-T) Research Group
Department of Electrical Engineering and Computer Science, Vanderbilt University
Nashville, TN, USA

Abstract - *Despite the numerous advantages of nanometer technologies, the increase in complexity also introduces a viable vector for attacking an integrated circuit (IC): a hardware attack, also known as a hardware Trojan. Since such an attack is implemented within the hardware of a design, it is generally undetectable to any software operating on this circuitry. To make matters worse, a hardware attack could be introduced at almost any point in a design's development cycle, be it through third-party intellectual property (IP) licensed for a design, or through unknown modifications made during the fabrication process. This malicious hardware could act as a kill-switch for a vital device, or as a data-leak for sensitive information. Activation would occur at some predetermined time or by a trigger from a malicious agent. An effective method is required to find such unexpected functionality. This paper describes several key challenges to be addressed in order to provide hardware assurance for trustworthy systems. We examine the platform of field programmable gate arrays (FPGAs) both for their potential vulnerability to threats within third-party IP as well as their capability to accelerate the testing of those modules.*

Keywords: Trusted hardware; malicious hardware detection; security; FPGAs; third-party intellectual property (IP)

1 Introduction

Trustworthy computing (with software) cannot exist until there is trustworthy hardware on which to build it [1]. To most designers, one of the advantages to implementing a design in hardware instead of as a software implementation is the secure nature of hardware. The assumption is prevalent that hardware is secure while software can be attacked. Unfortunately, this is a false assumption, created due to a lack of security awareness with increasingly complicated circuits. Advancements in process technology provide designers with the ability to put more transistors on a single silicon die [2] to fabricate increasingly complex designs. Unfortunately, the contents of these chips can be obscured, leading to potential security vulnerabilities within the hardware. A full design could have logical blocks contributed by dozens of different sources, with hundreds of different people contributing to the overall design. In some cases, these designers may have nothing to do with each other, and may come from outside of the company. There exists the threat that malicious agents can compromise the supply chain of integrated circuits (ICs) [3, 4] by inserting hardware Trojans (i.e., tiny circuits implanted in the original design to make it work contrary to the expected way in certain rare and critical situations [5]). In addition, the capital investment required for semiconductor foundries has limited the number of companies who fabricate their own ICs. Many companies have become "fabless" and rely upon overseas foundries to manufacture their designs (Table 1); these designs are then returned as packaged chips. The challenge of detecting malicious hardware requires that the testing methodology identifies unknown functionality within a chip after fabrication.

Table 1: 2011 Top 10 Semiconductor Foundries [6]

Rank	Foundry	Location	Sales (USD)
1	TSMC	Taiwan	14,533M
2	UMC	Taiwan	3,604M
3	GlobalFoundries	U.S.	3,580M
4	SMIC	China	1,319M
5	TowerJazz	Israel	613M
6	IBM Microelectronics	U.S.	545M
7	Vanguard International	Taiwan	516M
8	Dongbu HiTek	South Korea	483M
9	Samsung	South Korea	470M
10	Powerchip Technology	Taiwan	431M

Furthermore, different points of insertion can also involve different types of Trojans. A Trojan inserted at fabrication might utilize direct physical changes, due to the lack of a digital copy of the Trojan. On the other hand, a Trojan inserted through third-party intellectual property (IP) could pretend to be a type of digital watermark, yet hide additional malicious functionality. The reuse of IP makes it difficult to guarantee the security of a system when the underlying components are untrusted [7]. For example, a design might include licensed design modules from vendors supplying third-party intellectual property, requiring techniques to ensure the trustworthiness of those modules [8-11]. For reconfigurable systems using field-programmable gate arrays (FPGAs), third-party IP becomes a likely attack vector. Some approaches with FPGAs attempt to isolate modules within the system's implementation [12], or establish a root of trust within the FPGA fabric [13].

The concept of trust requires an accepted dependence or reliance upon another component or system [14]. In an age where hardware complexity provides the means to hide malicious hardware, the assumption that the hardware is secure can be misleading. Although software attacks are still the most common, a hardware attack emerges within the realm of possibility. Standard verification techniques ensures that a design meets the minimum functional requirements, but new methods of verification are required to guarantee that a design performs its intended function but nothing more. This paper discusses the challenges of developing trustworthy, reconfigurable computing systems. It is crucial for a designer to determine the trustworthiness of the design, as well as what possibilities are available for compromising that design. A solution for hardware assurance likely needs some automation to cover the potential test vector space. Reconfigurable hardware offers the possibility to accelerate the process.

The rest of this paper is organized as follows. Section 2 discusses hardware assurance and the basis for a root of trust. Section 3 provides a perspective on risk management by vendors and designers. Section 4 describes detection methods that have been developed and presented in the literature. Section 5 proposes a potential hardware testbed where field-programmable gate arrays (FPGAs) could be used to accelerate the verification process. Finally Section 6 summarizes the paper and offers some potential directions for future research.

2   Hardware Assurance

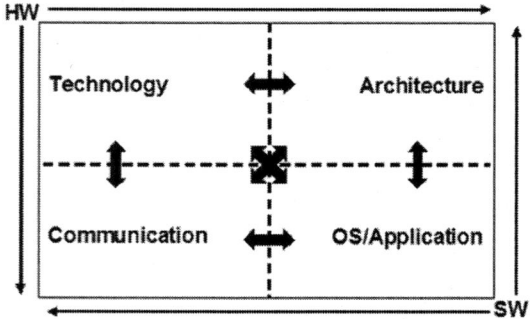

Figure 1: Linkages among hardware and software for secure and reliable computing

Many systems use hardware as the root of trust in order to defend against software-level attacks. Consequently, there is significant research on software assurance. However, viewing the system strictly in terms of hardware and software is a coarse-grained analysis. Understanding the linkages among technology, architecture, communication, and the application domain is critical for development of a trusted system (Figure 1). This section discusses the threat model used and its potential to affect full computing systems. It also describes a taxonomy for understanding malicious hardware and its potential impact on semiconductor intellectual property.

2.1   Threat model

One of the most insidious methods of attacking a circuit is by modifying its hardware in a malicious way. To put it simply, a hardware Trojan is created by discreetly inserting hidden functionality into a hardware design. This insertion can occur at any stage in a production path, and could have devastating effects on the final design. Such Trojans can have a variety of functionality, ranging from denial-of-service functionality that gives designs a controllable kill switch, to hidden data-leaks that can leak sensitive information [14].

One of the earliest papers covering the concept of Hardware Trojans was published by a group of researchers at the University of Champaign-Urbana [15]. This research included the design and test of a variant of the Aeroflex Gaisler LEON 3 [16] processor, called the Illinois Malicious Processor (IMP). The IMP was a fully functional version of the LEON 3 that operated normally in almost all circumstances, with the sole exception of one trigger: the receipt of a specially crafted corrupt network packet. Triggering this functionality would then switch the processor into a new shadow mode where the processor would accept and perform commands sent over the network. The shadow mode allowed an attacker to both compromise and hijack a system running on this processor, regardless of any security measures in the software. Additionally, this modification only required the insertion of 1,341 gates to the existing circuit, which originally contained over 1 million. Detecting such an insertion representing 0.1% of the circuit poses a significant problem. Even in much smaller circuits, the percent impact of hardware Trojans on the total area of a circuit is less than 0.5% [17, 18].

2.2   Classification of malicious hardware

The structure of a hardware Trojan can vary greatly depending upon intended functionality and payload [19]. A well-placed bug in a critical location can be as detrimental as a secret data-leak in a strong cryptosystem. Some Trojans are triggered via a specific sequence of inputs that are unlikely to occur in standard operation, and other Trojans are continuously active with an indiscernible payload. A taxonomy proposed by Karri et al. (Figure 2) [20] organizes Trojans based on 5 characteristics: (1) the point at which the Trojan enters the design, (2) the abstraction level of the Trojan, (3) the type of triggering which activates the Trojan, (4) the effect/payload of the Trojan, and (5) the location of the Trojan in the design. A similar taxonomy proposed by Wang et al. [21] focuses on three factors: (1) the physical characteristics (i.e., structure), (2) the activation characteristics (i.e., trigger), and (3) the action characteristics

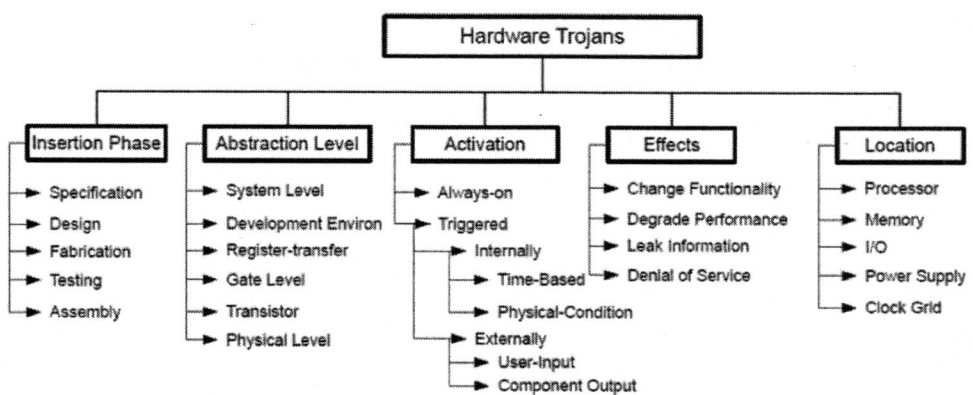

Figure 2: Hardware Trojan taxonomy based on five different attributes [20]

(i.e., payload). Additionally, while a large number of attacks fall under the classification of a hardware Trojan, the detection techniques are greatly dependent upon the individual characteristics of such Trojans.

2.3 Impact on semiconductor intellectual property (IP)

Depending on the method through which a Trojan is inserted, possible detection methods vary greatly [22-24]. Semiconductor IP has become a key part of electronics design because it can reduce IC development costs, accelerate time-to-market, reduce time-to-volume, and increase end-product value [25]. (According to Gartner Dataquest, the semiconductor IP market will reach $2.3B in 2014 [26].) Another confounding factor that increases the difficulty of developing countermeasures is that few attacks have been found in the wild. Instead, researchers must rely upon example attacks developed as benchmarks to illustrate the threat of malicious hardware. Unfortunately, these example attacks can often contain unnecessary functionality, making the detection of such an attack significantly easier. To make progress in this research area, it is necessary to understand both the attack and the defense of digital designs [27]. The Trust-Hub research community [28] developed as a forum to host and exchange resources related to hardware security and trust. It has grown to contain a significant number of tools and benchmarks, becoming the largest repository of hardware Trojans available to the public. It is supported by the National Science Foundation (NSF) and continually grows each year as contributors submit further resources.

3 Risk Management in the Supply Chain

When determining the security of a design, the first step is to identify clearly what types of steps in the design flow can be trusted, and what cannot. This determination might change depending upon the types of circuits and their implementations, but typically a vendor will trust its in-house design process and acknowledge the potential vulnerability of

external design. Of course, there is the possibility of insider threats [29, 30].

3.1 In-house design

A simplifying assumption made for the purpose of this discussion is that that all in-house design can be considered trusted. Under no circumstances does this mean that there are no security leaks, attempted sabotage, theft, or other problems within an organization. In fact, organizations have experienced this type of in-house threat. However, there are effective methods to resolve these threats that can be put into place. It is difficult to sabotage a design secretly if all changes to a digital design are tracked and logged with significant oversight on all changes. To put it simply, in-house design has its own process of verification that acts completely separately from other types of verification. The point of this assumption is to clearly define external attack vectors in order to most effectively block possible attacks. This allows a designer to guarantee that every possible step in a design is covered from attacks.

3.2 External design

After declaring all in-house work as trusted, the next step is to declare all work done outside of an organization as suspect. Any production step in which a design is modified by or in the care of an outside source can represent a possible vector for an attack. For each step, it is important to identify what attacks might be made by a third-party during this opportunity, and determine methods of either preventing or identifying such attacks. For example, a medical device company designing a pacemaker might license a wireless controller block from a vendor marketing third-party intellectual property (IP). It could be disastrous if this controller had malicious functionality hidden by the designer. In such a situation, it is foremost to identify the risk posed by incorporating this untrusted block in a design.

3.3   Vulnerabilities in the supply chain

One reason that external resources are considered universally untrusted is because of the difficulty in tracking the source of an external resource in the supply chain, regardless of the accompanying documentation. This has been a significant issue with defense contractors in the past few years, with regards to actual physical chips often purchased from reputable vendors or resellers. For example, a fiasco involving the United States Navy was made public in 2010, when a company called VisionTech was charged with selling over 59,000 microchips that contained hidden kill-switch functionality. This functionality would allow an attacker to disable whatever was running on these chips, including missiles, communication equipment, and other military vehicles. For years, this company had been importing counterfeit chips from China, and marketing them to defense companies as military grade microchips [31]. The list of these companies included: (1) BAE systems, which provided Identification Friend-or-Foe (IFF) systems to the U.S. Navy, and (2) Raytheon Missile systems, which supplied chips for use on F-16 fighter planes. Unfortunately, VisionTech is not the only reseller to buy cheap microchips from overseas and sell them domestically. Another similar example of corruption in the supply chain is the 2005 example of United Aircraft and Electronics, a company in which the operator was sentenced to 188 months in prison for false certification of aircraft parts sold [32]. Another 2002 example was the case of United Space Alliance, a company which bid and received a $24 million contract with NASA to supply military grade 8086 microprocessors for use with the space shuttle computers. This company then proceeded to purchase used computers off eBay and pull commercial-grade 8086 processors off the motherboards [32]. Commercial-grade chips would almost certainly have difficulties operating in the adverse environments required by the space shuttle computers. Unless it is possible to completely track the life of a resource, then that resource should be considered suspect. Since verification of an external resource is generally a simpler task than a full forensic investigation of the history of a resource, verification is the preferred method of determining whether something can be considered trusted.

4   Detection Methods

The majority of the existing methods proposed for identifying malicious hardware use the fabricated device; they can be classified into two types: (1) methods that detect changes on the transient current response drawn from extra circuitry on the chip [33-35], and (2) methods that detect timing differences due to the additional circuitry on the chip [36, 37]. A golden chip must be used as the trustworthy baseline in order to measure the deviation by a suspected chip. These methods assume that a trustworthy chip has already been identified, but do not address the issue of how to identify that chip in the first place. There are also some approaches that have attempted to encode signature information (i.e., a watermark) into the design to prevent

unwanted piracy of ICs [38-40] or use side-channel measurements to determine the signature of a design [33, 41]. In addition, fault injection could be used to provide hardware assurance [42].

4.1   Physical testing

After the fabrication stage, the individual packaged chips are subjected to a large amount of testing in order to make sure that the designs work as intended. This step can be very involved, depending upon the complexity of the chip. This can require expensive testing equipment and a significant investment of time in order to fully verify a circuit. While this step can be done entirely in-house, outsourcing it to save costs would introduce an opportunity for an attacker to replace chips with compromised ones. Generally, the test vectors chosen will be completely trusted. The test sequences can be chosen entirely in-house, and can be supplied entirely from a known trusted ATPG algorithm. Physical testing typically requires a golden copy of the design and sensitive measurement equipment. Even then, there are still challenges due to the potential of process variation that masks the response [43]. Another method of testing/authentication involves the use of physical unclonable functions (PUFs) to provide challenge/response pairs for a design's implementation [44, 45]. In order for a Trojan to remain hidden, there are three main characteristics that directly contribute to the difficulty of identification. If even one of these characteristics is lacking, then the difficulty in detecting the Trojan will be reduced.

Small Size: As Trojans can be constructed using a fraction of a percent of the components in the overall circuit, they can be quite small and still attain the desired functionality. However, the larger the Trojan grows, the more circuitry is added to the circuit, thus affecting its functionality. Even if the Trojan is not triggered, some inputs can activate smaller sections of the Trojan, changing the power consumed by the chip. Some techniques involve partially activating the Trojan circuitry in order to make it easier to detect [46, 47]. Additional circuitry is also more likely to displace the existing circuitry, compromising the second desired characteristic of hardware Trojans.

Low Displacement: When inserting a Trojan, it can be necessary to relocate existing circuitry, in order to make room for malicious components. However, such displacement of existing components can have a significant effect on side-channel measurements, making it possible to detect the malicious circuitry [22, 33, 35, 36]. In some cases, a very small Trojan added to a circuit could have a significant effect on the timing response of a circuit, especially if an automatic place-and-route function is implemented. In this case, manual placement of the Trojan circuitry in the layout can minimize the displacement of existing circuitry and help the Trojan to remain covert.

Resistance to unintended triggering: The last characteristic necessary for a Trojan to remain undiscovered is simply for it to be difficult to trigger accidentally. It does not matter how large the Trojan is, or how artfully placed the

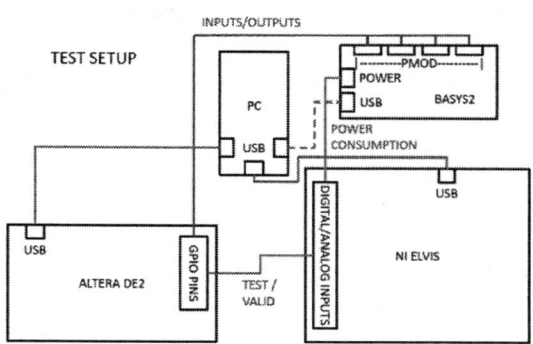

Figure 3: Test setup using an FPGA to provide input test vectors and monitor the output

components are if the Trojan is found during routine testing, such as standard logical verification. If the Trojan is always on and lacks a trigger, then the payload needs to be something discreet that does not appear on standard tests. For example, the Trojan in the modified LEON3 processor [15] was triggered via a uniquely crafted network packet, which would normally be treated as corrupt. Such a possible input would likely never be tested, simply because it is impossible to test every possible input on every possible state. However, this inability to test every possible input is what makes hardware Trojans effective as malicious attacks.

4.2 Third-party IP

As third-party IP is supplied from an external source, there is no baseline with which to compare the IP to in order to identify differences. Instead, it becomes necessary to identify possibly suspicious behavior in a design. This means that the IP design needs to be thoroughly analyzed for possible malicious functionality. Thus, the most significant vector to attacking a circuit during the design stage comes through the inclusion of third-party IP in a design. Most organizations cannot afford to re-invent solutions every time a common component is used, and therefore rely on IP vendors that supply design-modules to perform the desired functionality. The organization can save money and time while avoiding the issue of creating the design from scratch. Designers will instead assemble licensed design modules in order to meet the design specification, often treating the third-party IP as black boxes. These unknown designs can easily make their way unmodified into a final design, allowing for an effective vector for compromising a circuit.

Suppose that a designer were to license a cryptographic circuit for use within a design. The cryptographic block's encryption could be easily undermined if it were to possess an extra hidden key. While it would appear to function correctly under normal use, someone with knowledge of the hidden key could easily circumvent any security provided by the cryptographic block within the final design. Another risk with third-party IP is that there are a plethora of vendors supplying designs for every possible function, with very little oversight.

Vendors come and go, often only possessing an online presence. It would not be difficult for a malicious agent to create a fake vendor persona, and supply malicious design modules at a below-market fee. Compounding the problem is the continuous issue of stolen IP design modules. Vendors sometimes have their IP stolen and resold by other vendors, or even just stolen by designers wanting to use the IP for free. Unfortunately, this has led to a culture of obfuscation and suspicion, making it difficult to get clean, non-obfuscated code in order to identify possible attacks.

5 Accelerated Testing with FPGAs

Although FPGAs exhibit vulnerabilities to the insertion of malicious hardware, they do offer the potential to assist with detecting threats within a design. FPGAs could be used in fault injection campaigns to identify suspected behavior within a design. The potential test vector space is very large, when considering: (1) the number of input vectors (2) the number of fault locations, and (3) the current state for a particular cycle of operation. Emulation in hardware would require less time than using traditional simulation tools [42]. FPGA hardware can also be used to perform the testing in an automated manner. Figure 3 shows a test setup to measure the power drawn for a design under test (DUT). The DUT is a Xilinx BASYS2 FPGA development board, and the I/O is supplied by an Altera DE2 FPGA development board.

6 Summary and Future Work

Unfortunately, detecting malicious hardware within a reconfigurable computing system is an exceedingly difficult task. Inactive Trojans can have an exceedingly small impact on a circuit in terms of area and power, and Trojans are statistically unlikely to be triggered on accident. Stealth is also a key requirement of malicious hardware. A reliance on third-party IP offers a direct path for the insertion of malicious hardware. The very nature of reconfigurability with FPGAs opens the door for security vulnerabilities. Despite the evident need for detecting such changes to a circuit design, there is currently no simple solution to this problem. Many methods wait until after a chip is fabricated. One alternative is to take samples of the lot for extensive analysis. However, examining the die is becoming increasingly more difficult as transistors decrease in size. Even with an expensive imaging procedure, it would not be possible to test every chip ordered, as imaging may require the destruction of the chip. Other techniques involve detecting changes in the electric current drawn from extra circuitry on the chip, or detecting timing differences due to the additional circuitry on the chip. These methods rely upon the characterization of a golden copy in their comparison, but this trustworthy copy is not available if the original design was compromised, or the parameters could be masked due to process variation on the IC. This paper described the key research challenges for identifying malicious hardware and the state-of-the-art for detection and verification. Yet, there are still opportunities for research contributions as new application domains emerge. For example, in FPGA-based software-defined radio, a designer must defend against malicious modification during initialization and runtime [48]. In wireless sensor networks, the need security emerges for access/discovery, routing, and information [49]. Hardware/software codesign [50] also offers the potential to include security within the overall design framework to address the linkages among technology, architecture, communication, and applications for trustworthy reconfigurable systems.

7   Acknowledgment

This work was supported in part by TRUST (The Team for Research in Ubiquitous Secure Technology), which receives support from the National Science Foundation (NSF award number CCF-0424422) and the following organizations: AFOSR (#FA9550-06-1-0244) Cisco, British Telecom, ESCHER, HP, IBM, iCAST, Intel, Microsoft, ORNL, Pirelli, Qualcomm, Sun, Symantec, Telecom Italia and United Technologies.

8   References

[1] D. Collins, "DARPA "TRUST in IC's" effort," in *Microsystems Technology Symposium*, San Jose, CA, 2007.

[2] G. E. Moore, "Cramming more components onto integrated circuits," *Proceedings of the IEEE*, vol. 86, pp. 82-85, 1998.

[3] S. Adee, "The hunt for the kill switch," *IEEE Spectrum*, vol. 45, pp. 34-39, 2008.

[4] M. Inman. (2008). *Malicious hardware may be next hacker tool*. Available: http://www.newscientist.com/article/mg19826546.000-malicious-hardware-may-be-next-hacker-tool.html

[5] M. Banga, "Partition based approaches for the isolation and detection of embedded trojans in ICs," Master of Science Master of Science, Electrical and Computer Engineering, Virginia Polytechnic Institute and State University, Blacksburg, VA, 2008.

[6] Solid State Technology. (2012). *Top 10 semiconductor foundries in 2011*. Available: http://www.electroiq.com/articles/sst/2012/03/top-10-semiconductor-foundries-in-2011.html

[7] P. Kocher, R. Lee, G. McGraw, A. Raghunathan, and S. Ravi, "Security as a new dimension in embedded system design," in *41st Design Automation Conference (DAC 2004)*, San Diego, CA, 2004, pp. 753-760.

[8] E. Love, J. Yier, and Y. Makris, "Enhancing security via provably trustworthy hardware intellectual property," in *2011 IEEE International Symposium on Hardware-Oriented Security and Trust (HOST)*, 2011, pp. 12-17.

[9] E. Love, J. Yier, and Y. Makris, "Proof-carrying hardware intellectual property: A pathway to trusted module acquisition," *IEEE Transactions on Information Forensics and Security*, vol. 7, pp. 25-40, 2012.

[10] T. Reece, D. B. Limbrick, and W. H. Robinson, "Design comparison to identify malicious hardware in external intellectual property," in *2011 IEEE 10th International Conference on Trust, Security and Privacy in Computing and Communications (TrustCom)*, Changsha, China, 2011, pp. 639-646.

[11] G. Shrestha and M. S. Hsiao, "Ensuring trust of third-party hardware design with constrained sequential equivalence checking," in *2012 IEEE Conference on Technologies for Homeland Security (HST)*, 2012, pp. 7-12.

[12] T. Huffmire, B. Brotherton, W. Gang, T. Sherwood, R. Kastner, T. Levin, T. Nguyen, and C. Irvine, "Moats and drawbridges: An isolation primitive for reconfigurable hardware based systems," in *IEEE Symposium on Security and Privacy (SP '07)*, 2007, pp. 281-295.

[13] T. Eisenbarth, T. Güneysu, C. Paar, A.-R. Sadeghi, D. Schellekens, and M. Wolf, "Reconfigurable trusted computing in hardware," in *2007 ACM Workshop on Scalable Trusted Computing*, Alexandria, VA, USA, 2007, pp. 15-20.

[14] C. E. Irvine and K. Levitt, "Trusted hardware: Can it be trustworthy?" in *44th ACM/IEEE Design Automation Conference (DAC '07)*, 2007, pp. 1-4.

[15] S. T. King, J. Tucek, A. Cozzie, C. Grier, W. Jiang, and Y. Zhou, "Designing and implementing malicious hardware," in *1st Usenix Workshop on Large-Scale Exploits and Emergent Threats (LEET 2008)*, San Francisco, CA, 2008.

[16] J. Gaisler and M. Isomäki, "LEON3 GR-XC3S-1500 Template Design," ed: Gaisler Research, 2006.

[17] T. Reece, D. B. Limbrick, X. Wang, B. T. Kiddie, and W. H. Robinson, "Stealth assessment of hardware trojans in a microcontroller," in *30th IEEE International Conference on Computer Design (ICCD 2012)*, Montreal, Quebec, Canada, 2012.

[18] T. Reece and W. H. Robinson, "Analysis of data-leak hardware Trojans in AES cryptographic circuits," in *IEEE*

Conference on Technologies for Homeland Security (HST '13), Waltham, MA, 2013.

[19] M. Tehranipoor and F. Koushanfar, "A survey of hardware trojan taxonomy and detection," *IEEE Design & Test of Computers*, vol. 27, pp. 10-25, 2010.

[20] R. Karri, J. Rajendran, K. Rosenfeld, and M. Tehranipoor, "Trustworthy hardware: Identifying and classifying hardware trojans," *Computer*, vol. 43, pp. 39-46, 2010.

[21] X. Wang, M. Tehranipoor, and J. Plusquellic, "Detecting malicious inclusions in secure hardware: Challenges and solutions," in *IEEE International Workshop on Hardware-Oriented Security and Trust (HOST 2008)*, 2008, pp. 15-19.

[22] F. Koushanfar and A. Mirhoseini, "A unified framework for multimodal submodular integrated circuits trojan detection," *IEEE Transactions on Information Forensics and Security*, vol. 6, pp. 162-174, 2011.

[23] H. Salmani and M. Tehranipoor, "Layout-aware switching activity localization to enhance hardware trojan detection," *IEEE Transactions on Information Forensics and Security*, vol. 7, pp. 76-87, 2012.

[24] H. Salmani, M. Tehranipoor, and J. Plusquellic, "A novel technique for improving hardware trojan detection and reducing trojan activation time," *IEEE Transactions on Very Large Scale Integration (VLSI) Systems*, vol. 20, pp. 112-125, 2012.

[25] V. Ratford, N. Popper, D. Caldwell, and T. Katsioulas, "Understanding the semiconductor intellectual property (SIP) business process," in *SIP Handbook*, ed: Fabless Semiconductor Association, 2003.

[26] J. Koeter. *What's Next in Semiconductor IP?* Available: http://www.gabeoneda.com/news/what%E2%80%99s-next-semiconductor-ip

[27] T. Reece and W. H. Robinson, "Hardware Trojans: The defense and attack of integrated circuits," in *29th IEEE International Conference on Computer Design (ICCD 2011)*, Amherst, MA, 2011, pp. 293-296.

[28] *trust-HUB*. Available: http://trust-hub.org/

[29] A. Waksman and S. Sethumadhavan, "Tamper evident microprocessors," in *2010 IEEE Symposium on Security and Privacy (SP)*, 2010, pp. 173-188.

[30] A. Waksman and S. Sethumadhavan, "Silencing hardware backdoors," in *2011 IEEE Symposium on Security and Privacy (SP)*, 2011, pp. 49-63.

[31] Department of Justice Press Release. (2011). *Administrator of VisionTech Components, LLC sentenced to 38 months in prison for her role in sales of counterfeit integrated circuits destined to U.S. military and other industries.* Available: http://www.justice.gov/usao/dc/news/2011/oct/11-472.html

[32] J. Stradley and D. Karraker, "The electronic part supply chain and risks of counterfeit parts in defense applications," *IEEE Transactions on Components and Packaging Technologies*, vol. 29, pp. 703-705, 2006.

[33] D. Agrawal, S. Baktir, D. Karakoyunlu, P. Rohatgi, and B. Sunar, "Trojan detection using IC fingerprinting," in *IEEE Symposium on Security and Privacy (SP '07)*, 2007, pp. 296-310.

[34] R. Rad, J. Plusquellic, and M. Tehranipoor, "Sensitivity analysis to hardware trojans using power supply transient signals," in *IEEE International Workshop on Hardware-Oriented Security and Trust (HOST 2008)*, 2008, pp. 3-7.

[35] X. Wang, H. Salmani, M. Tehranipoor, and J. Plusquellic, "Hardware trojan detection and isolation using current integration and localized current analysis," in *IEEE International Symposium on Defect and Fault Tolerance of VLSI Systems (DFTVS '08)*, 2008, pp. 87-95.

[36] Y. Jin and Y. Makris, "Hardware trojan detection using path delay fingerprint," in *IEEE International Workshop on Hardware-Oriented Security and Trust (HOST 2008)*, 2008, pp. 51-57.

[37] J. Li and J. Lach, "At-speed delay characterization for IC authentication and trojan horse detection," in *IEEE International Workshop on Hardware-Oriented Security and Trust (HOST 2008)*, 2008, pp. 8-14.

[38] F. Koushanfar, I. Hong, and M. Potkonjak, "Behavioral synthesis techniques for intellectual property protection," *ACM Transactions on Design Automation of Electronic Systems (TODAES)*, vol. 10, pp. 523-545, 2005.

[39] Y. Alkabani, F. Koushanfar, N. Kiyavash, and M. Potkonjak, "Trusted integrated circuits: A nondestructive hidden characteristics extraction approach," in *Information Hiding*. vol. 5284, ed: Springer Berlin Heidelberg, 2008, pp. 102-117.

[40] J. A. Roy, F. Koushanfar, and I. L. Markov, "Ending piracy of integrated circuits," *Computer*, vol. 43, pp. 30-38, 2010.

[41] S. Sathyanarayana, W. H. Robinson, and R. A. Beyah, "A novel network-based approach to counterfeit detection," in *IEEE Conference on Technologies for Homeland Security (HST '13)*, Waltham, MA, 2013.

[42] H. M. Quinn, D. A. Black, W. H. Robinson, and S. P. Buchner, "Fault simulation and emulation tools to augment radiation-hardness assurance testing," *IEEE Transactions on Nuclear Science*, vol. 60, pp. 2119-2142, 2013.

[43] S. G. Narendra, "Challenges and design choices in nanoscale CMOS," *Journal of Emerging Technology in Computer Systems*, vol. 1, pp. 7-49, 2005.

[44] B. Gassend, D. Clarke, M. v. Dijky, and S. Devadas, "Silicon physical random functions," in *9th ACM Conference on Computer and Communications Security*, Washington, DC, USA, 2002, pp. 148 - 160.

78

Int'l Conf. Reconfigurable Systems and Algorithms | ERSA'13 |

[45] M. Majzoobi, F. Koushanfar, and M. Potkonjak, "Techniques for design and implementation of secure reconfigurable PUFs," *ACM Transactions on Reconfigurable Technology and Systems*, vol. 2, pp. 1-33, 2009.

[46] M. Banga and M. S. Hsiao, "A region based approach for the identification of hardware trojans," in *IEEE International Workshop on Hardware-Oriented Security and Trust (HOST 2008)*, 2008, pp. 40-47.

[47] M. Banga and M. S. Hsiao, "A novel sustained vector technique for the detection of hardware trojans," in *22nd International Conference on VLSI Design*, New Delhi, India, 2009, pp. 327-332.

[48] C. Li, N. K. Jha, and A. Raghunathan, "Secure reconfiguration of software-defined radio," *ACM Transactions on Embedded Computing Systems*, vol. 11, pp. 1-22, 2012.

[49] J. Yick, B. Mukherjee, and D. Ghosal, "Wireless sensor network survey," *Computer Networks*, vol. 52, pp. 2292-2330, 2008.

[50] J. Teich, "Hardware/Software Codesign: The past, the present, and predicting the future," *Proceedings of the IEEE*, vol. 100, pp. 1411-1430, 2012.

Author Index